# "Wealth Code" UNLOCKED

**(Faith, Real Estate, and Seeing What Other's Cannot)**

**By**

**Dr. Leon K. McCray**

"Beloved, I wish above all things that thou mayest prosper and be in health, even as thy soul prospereth." – (3 John 2)

 ISBN: ISBN: 979-8-9944832-0-6

Unless otherwise indicated, all Scriptural quotations are taken from the King James Version of the Bible. Printed in the United States of America

Printed by Lighthouse Legacy Publishing

Disclaimer

This book is for educational, informational, and inspirational purposes only. The author has made every effort to ensure the accuracy of the information presented herein; however, he makes no representations or warranties regarding the completeness, reliability, or suitability of this material for your particular situation.

This book does not constitute legal, tax, financial, investment, real estate, or professional advice. Readers are encouraged to consult with qualified professionals – such as licensed financial advisors, attorneys, tax professionals, or real estate experts – before making any decisions based on the principles or strategies discussed in these pages.

The personal stories, examples, and testimonies are shared for illustration and motivational purposes. Individual results will vary, and past performance is not a guarantee of future outcomes. The author and publisher expressly disclaim any liability for any direct or indirect loss, risk, or damages incurred as a consequence of the use or application of the contents of this book.

Faith-based references, biblical teachings, and scriptural insights are provided as spiritual encouragement and should not be interpreted as a substitute for professional or personal judgment.

By reading this book, you acknowledge and accept full responsibility for your actions, choices, and results.

---

# Endorsements

**"Wealth Code" Unlocked** is more than a book, it's a transformational deposit of wisdom and revelation. It is a divine blueprint that awakens vision, ignites purpose and empower transformation. This book is a prophetic manual for breakthroughs. Within these pages, the author masterfully reveals timeless principles that shift paradigms, challenge limitations, unlock destinies and release abundance into every area of life.

This is more than information, it is impartation, birthed from vision and poured out with passion. Readers will not only discover keys to financial wealth but also to spiritual wholeness, generational legacy, and Kingdom impact.

I honor and celebrate Apostle, Dr. Leon K. McCray for courageously depositing such a life-changing resource into the hands of the world. He skillfully equips readers with principles that change mindset and challenge them to walk in the abundance and favor of God. If you are ready to embrace God's best and unlock your true potential this is the book you have been waiting for! ***Apostle, Dr. Tony Barhoo – Senior Pastor & Founder of Living Faith World Ministries***

---

Dr. Leon K. McCray provides a current and effective plan in **"Wealth Code" Unlocked** for overcoming financial obstacles and achieving Kingdom prosperity. His biblically grounded and practically applicable insights enable readers to change their perspective and accept God's abundant provision. This book is about discovering your divine destiny and leading an impactful life. To any believer who wants to enter God's best, I heartily endorse it. ***Bishop Benny & Dr E Daniels, Benny Daniels International, CEO/Founder***

---

"Wealth Code" Unlocked is anchored in Scripture and guided by financial literacy. Its transformative insights are both captivating and practical. A remarkable work – and a must-read for anyone seeking a disciplined approach to investing or understanding the psychology of money."
***Shirley Smith, Vice President Banker***

The **"Wealth Code" Unlocked** doesn't just teach you how to build wealth - it unlocks your identity, purpose, and legacy. It's part financial playbook, part Kingdom blueprint, and 100% a-call to action. Read it, move on it, and watch your life multiply. This book is more than words on a page - it's a blueprint for transformation. Leon doesn't just inspire; he equips you with practical strategies rooted in faith, mindset, and stewardship. He shows how true wealth begins in the mind and flows into action, offering real-life stories and biblical principles that make you pause, reflect, and move. If you're ready to stop consuming information and start implementing strategies that build both financial legacy and Kingdom impact, this is the guide you've been waiting for. ***Mike Ealy, President Nassau Investments***

---

The **"Wealth Code" Unlocked:** What a blessing and powerful book Apostle Dr. Leon K. McCray has written. He has not only written a book, but he has literally poured his life into this book. Having had the honor and privilege to serve the Lord with him and visit some of his properties, I am a first-hand witness of his unselfishness in sharing the secrets of his success. Whether from a spiritual angle or a professional angle, both are accommodated in this book. This book is a must read for anyone who genuinely wants to make a shift in wealth creation, and I wholeheartedly endorse it. **Bishop Tom Alex Ominde,** ***Presiding Bishop and General Overseer, House of Favour Worship Churches, Nairobi Kenya***

---

"The author has invited his readers into the sacred journey of discovering God's purpose in his life. With unwavering obedience and a relentless commitment to follow the Lord, he pressed through the darkness until truth was unveiled in the light. That journey is reflected throughout these pages. As Jesus said, 'The mystery of the Kingdom of God has been given to you who have teachable hearts" *(Mark 4:11, AMP)*. The "Wealth Code" Unlocked is such a mystery revealed. This is a must-read for every Kingdom citizen!"
***Pastors Randall & Jennifer Griggs, Senior Pastors, Tree of Kingdom Life Ministries, Woodbridge, VA***

---

"I have had the privilege of walking closely with Dr. Leon McCray through seasons of both challenge and triumph. What he shares in this book is not theory, but hard-won truth – principles birthed in the fire of experience and proven by results. The revelations contained here are Kingdom keys that, when applied, bring real transformation. I know, because I've seen their impact in my own life. This is not a 'get-rich-quick' message, but a divine invitation to walk in greater intimacy with God, and to hear His voice. This is a must-read for those who want to unlock the treasures He has reserved for His people." ***Tony P. Harrison, Air Force Veteran/Friend for 40+ years***

---

This book is a true blessing for the body of Christ and the Kingdom of God. It reminds us that while tithing is an act of obedience and faith, it is only the beginning of living a life of abundance. With grace and clarity, the author teaches us how to faithfully manage and grow the 90%, stewarding our resources with honor, excellence, and authority. The insights shared here help remove the blinders and open our eyes to a new perspective of the abundance God has prepared for His people. Most importantly, it points us to the heart of God - helping us hear His voice and see what others have missed. This book will not only enrich your finances, but also your faith and walk with Father God. ***F. Michael King, DMin.***

"Dr. Leon McCray is one of the wisest men I have had the privilege of knowing in my own pursuit of greatness. *The "Wealth Code" Unlocked* is a must-read for those who feel weary from the grind, uncertain about tomorrow, or unclear about their next step in life or business. This book is not about chasing money; it's about unlocking your true purpose and aligning your mindset and faith with God's principles. Whether you are just starting out or have already achieved a measure of success yet feel directionless, the insights within these pages will guide you toward building not only wealth, but legacy. Think of it as a roadmap to abundance, prosperity, and purpose – one that only opens when you adopt the right mindset and Kingdom perspective. Once you apply what Dr. McCray shares, you will discover the "Wealth Code" Unlocked within you."
***Simon Miller, Chief Lending Officer, Endaxi Financial, Inc.***

---

"This book unlocks something deep within – a conviction that you cannot only accomplish but exceed any financial goals you have the faith to believe for. Guided by the Spirit of God, these teachings lead you down a path of wealth you may never have thought possible. Fear of failure is replaced with faith, and new confidence arises as you realize that prosperity has always been part of your Kingdom inheritance. *The "Wealth Code" Unlocked* equips you with the mindset, mentality, and motivation to manifest abundance at new levels. It's not just a must-read once, but again and again – because with every reading, another layer of identity, clarity, and purpose is revealed. Thank God for this book and thank God for Dr. Leon McCray!"
***Apostle, Glenn G. Hagler Ministries***

I have had the honor of knowing **Dr. Leon K. McCray** for over 15 years, and in that time, I have consistently witnessed him to be a man of integrity, vision, and great faith. As a successful businessman and leader, he not only lives by the principles he teaches but also has a genuine passion for unlocking the hidden potential in others.

In **"Wealth Code" Unlocked,** Dr. McCray goes beyond theory – he reveals practical principles and timeless wisdom that inspire readers to take bold action. This book is more than just a guide to financial success; it is a roadmap to purpose-driven achievement that empowers individuals to step into greater possibilities.

Dr. McCray has poured his experience, insight, and faith into these pages, and I believe every reader will walk away, equipped and motivated to pursue the next level of their destiny. ***Apostle Desiree Fox, Regional Leader, Christian International Apostolic Network, Mid-Atlantic Region***

# Dedication

***This book is lovingly dedicated to my wonderful mother Mrs. Margaret Brown*** – who I affectionately called "Sugar" (after I was grown, of course). I loved her so very much. She was more than a mother; she was a protector, a prayer warrior, and the truest example of God's love in action. To raise a boy like me, she had to pray – and pray she did. Her prayers were the covering that carried me through some of the most challenging seasons of my life. Even when I did not know how to pray for myself, she knew how to reach heaven on my behalf, and God honored her prayers in my life.

She was a God-fearing woman with a heart full of compassion. I watched her serve others with joy – bringing food to the elderly, visiting those who were shut in, and walking into nursing homes with a smile that carried hope. And she made sure I walked right beside her. At the time, I didn't realize it, but she was training me – shaping in me that same heart for people, that same love for service.

When I left home, it was her love and her prayers that kept me. In the midst of trials and in the face of adversity, I could feel her intercession wrapping around me like a shield. She had favor with God, and that favor extended to her son – and for that I am forever grateful.

I pray you knew the depth of my love for you. I miss you deeply. This book is dedicated to you, and to the God you served so faithfully, and to the Christ who lived so powerfully in you.

# TABLE OF CONTENTS

# Foreword

I first met Apostle Dr. Leon K. McCray over twenty years ago while serving as an itinerant prophet to the nations – ministering across more than twenty-two countries, representing the Kingdom of God before kings, presidents, and world leaders. During a season when the Lord instructed me to be still and seek His face, God divinely connected me with Dr. McCray and his precious wife, Dr. Valerie McCray. In that transition, they stood with me in prayer, encouragement, and tangible support, faithfully sowing into my life while I sought the Lord. They demonstrated the true principle of honoring and caring for a prophet of God.

On more than one occasion, the Lord allowed me to speak prophetically into Dr. McCray's life. I declared that he carried a prophetic and apostolic anointing in the realm of finance. His Kingdom assignment, I shared, would be to teach and train others in biblical wealth-building, to equip the Body of Christ as a Kingdom paymaster, and to author books and manuals on God's financial plans and strategies for both the church and the marketplace.

Today, I am humbled and proud to see that prophetic word fulfilled in this book, *The "Wealth Code" Unlocked.* Throughout the years I have known Dr. McCray, I have watched him live, manage, and operate according to the very principles and models he now teaches in these pages. His life and ministry are evidence that God has chosen him for this end-time season—to mentor and lead the Body of Christ apostolically in the arena of Kingdom finance.

The Holy Scriptures are full of divine patterns concerning money, stewardship, and increase. In His faithfulness, God has entrusted Dr. Leon McCray with revelation that crystallizes those truths into what he now calls *the "Wealth Code" Unlocked.* This book is not just information – it is impartation. It is a divine blueprint for those called to steward wealth with Kingdom purpose.

I recommend this book to you with all sincerity. Read it with an open heart and expect God to unlock within you the same wisdom, authority, and strategies that He has entrusted to His servant, Dr. Leon K. McCray.

**Apostle, Dr. Tony V. Robertson, MTh, Ph.D.** ***Founder, Spirit of Truth International Ministries, (S.P.O.T.tm), Washington, D.C.***

# Preface

There comes a moment in every person's life when they realize that what they've been taught about money, success, and purpose has only scratched the surface of what's truly possible. For me, that moment came years ago through an encounter with a book, a journey through Scripture, and a series of life experiences that forced me to either sink or rise higher in faith.

But what I didn't know then, and what you may not fully realize yet, is that wealth is not just about dollars and cents. It's about destiny. It's about identity. It's about **unlocking a divine code** that was written into your life before you ever took your first breath.

This book, ***the "Wealth Code" Unlocked***, is more than pages of financial strategies or inspirational words. It's a clarion call. It's a trumpet blast in the middle of uncertain times, summoning you to rise above fear, lack, and average living. It's an invitation to step boldly into the fullness of who you are in Christ and to see what others cannot see.

I didn't write this book to impress you with my journey. I wrote it because I believe with everything in me that you were created for more - more than bills, more than survival, and more than cycles of scarcity. You were created for abundance, impact, and legacy. And not just for yourself, but to transform families, communities, and nations through the wealth and wisdom God places in your hands.

I want you to read these chapters with an open heart and a sharp mind. Let the truths challenge you. Let the stories stir you. Let the strategies guide you. But most importantly, let the Spirit of God speak to you as you read. When you align faith, wisdom, and vision, you tap into a system of Kingdom multiplication that no recession, no crisis, and no opposition can shut down.

**This is your moment**. This is your invitation. This is the key in your hand. **Unlock the "Wealth Code"**. And once it's unlocked, walk boldly into the life, legacy, and destiny that were always meant to be yours.

*Dr. Leon K. McCray*

# Introduction

## Why This Book, Why Now – **This is your Clarion Call to Action**

---

### Faith, Real Estate, and Seeing What Others Cannot

---

This book didn't just come out of thin air. It's the result of decades of walking out real-life experiences, learning from both wins and setbacks, and carrying a conviction that I just couldn't shake.

I still remember it like it was yesterday. It was 1998 and I had just gotten married. During my time in Virginia, a gentleman I came to know and love as "Poppa Charles" handed me a book. It wasn't thick. It wasn't fancy. But it was powerful. The title: *Rich Dad Poor Dad* by Robert T. Kiyosaki.

That book rocked me! It opened my eyes to a new way of thinking about money and wealth. But here's where the real shift happened: It was when I took those principles and combined them with what I already knew from the Word of God. That's when everything in my life began to pivot. My mindset shifted. My perspective stretched. My faith aligned with financial wisdom. And from that moment on - the trajectory of my life and eventually my legacy was forever changed.

My prayer and my declaration for you is that *the "Wealth Code" Unlocked* will do the same for you. That as you read and apply what's in these pages, your thinking will expand, your mindset will shift, and you'll be propelled to the next level in your wealth-building and Kingdom-advancing journey.

Because here's the truth: the principles of wealth were never meant to be hidden from God's people. They were meant to be revealed, stewarded, and multiplied. Not just so you can prosper, but so the Kingdom can advance through you - and so you can leave a legacy that outlives you (that's my heart).

You could be reading any book right now. Why this one? **Because it's about you, not me**. I didn't write this to impress you with my journey. **I wrote it to empower you on yours** – financially, spiritually, and mentally.

Whether you're an aspiring or seasoned investor, entrepreneur, ministry leader, or builder of legacy – this **book is your roadmap. It's for those who sense there's more**… more to do, more to build, more to give, and more to become. You'll find mindset-shaping truths, real estate strategies, Kingdom economics, and spiritual insight. But even more than that, you'll find clarity about your identity and authority as a child of God.

We live in uncertain times. **While others panic, you can prosper** – but not by accident. It takes mindset, strategy, faith, and vision. God's Word works when we work it. And when you align your life with His principles, you unlock a system of favor, multiplication, and supernatural provision.

Inside these pages, **I'll share what I've learned from decades in the trenches**:

• How to develop a rich mindset that aligns with Kingdom truth
• How to master real estate principles in any market
• How to create multiple streams of passive income

• Why tithing by itself is **not** enough for living life in abundance
• How to faithfully manage and **GROW the 90%** that remains after giving
• How to steward money with honor, excellence, and authority
• How to break free from generational scarcity and embrace abundance
• How to hear God's voice and see what others cannot see

This book is more than just strategies – it's **one of my life's assignments**. I've lived this. I've survived storms, navigated recessions, rebuilt from failures, and discovered God's supernatural provision and guidance along the way.

I believe we perish not from a lack of opportunity – but from a lack of knowledge, faith, vision, and execution. **My mandate is to change that**.

So whether you're just starting or you've already built something meaningful – this **book will be your guide to unlocking the "Wealth Code" for the highest of Kingdom Level Blessings**.

**You have this book in your hand, so you are not average.** You were made in the image of a limitless God. And He has given you power to get wealth – not just for your gain, but for His Kingdom purpose.

**Backdrop: A Story of Identity, Legacy, and Love**

From my earliest days, I grew up with a man in my home who filled the role of Dad, the one who raised me with unwavering support, guidance, and consistency. **He wasn't the man who shared my DNA, but in every important way, he was my Dad**. He taught me right from wrong, celebrated my successes, and walked me through every storm.

Still, there remained a quiet space in my heart – a longing, a question mark that hovered over the story of my life.

Who was the one who gave me life?
Was he there in the hospital when I was born?
What did he think or feel when he saw me for the first time?

I had questions – not just out of curiosity, but because I sensed something deeper was hidden in the answers. It was as if secrets were written in my DNA, shaping the essence of who I was called to become. These questions weren't distractions – they **were puzzle pieces, missing from the mosaic of my identity**.

As I matured, the search for those answers didn't fade. Instead, it became a compass, guiding me through life's storms and decisions. I knew I was called to something greater, but I needed to find what was locked deep within. I didn't have language for it back then, but today I call it the **"Wealth Code" Unlocked**.

It wasn't just about money.
It was about identity.
It was about Love.
It was about purpose, legacy, and wholeness.

**Let me give you some context**.

My mother was a loving and resilient woman who poured her heart into raising her three children. I have an older brother, Glenn – who is the best brother on the planet – and a brilliant younger sister, Rene, or "Nae Nae," as I still affectionately call her today. Life was stable, but scarce. There was never enough food (meat to be specific), shoes, toys, or resources. Still, even in lack, I sensed an invisible abundance just beyond reach.

**Somewhere deep inside, I knew there was more**.

As a young man, I joined the military and found myself stationed at Holloman Air Force Base in New Mexico. It was there **I met a fellow airman – Airman Parker. I don't remember his first name, but if anyone reading this book knows him from Holloman AFB during the 1977–1978 timeframe, please help me reconnect**. I'm eternally grateful to him – for it was through him that I was finally introduced to my ***real Father**.

**That meeting was life-changing and destiny-defining**. I got answers to questions that had echoed in my mind for decades.

From that moment on, every encounter with my Father unlocked something deeper inside me – not just about Him, but about myself. Each story acted like a key, opening vaults of identity, healing, impartation, generational wisdom, and a wealthy mind-set.

**And that's when it hit me:**

**This is the true "Wealth Code" Unlocked".**

It's not just about finances and wealth **(though that's very important)**.
It's spiritual.
It's **generational**.
It's identity.
It's **purpose**.
It's dominion.
It's the **key to Unlock the "Wealth Code"**.

**Let's Go In and SEE.**

# Chapter 1

## The Bedrock of the "Wealth Code" Unlocked

## Faith & Mindset

---

Before we talk about strategies and numbers, let's talk to the One who owns it all. Take a slow breath. If you're comfortable, whisper your name – *I'm praying for you by name right now.* Then read this prayer out loud or quietly in your heart.

**Opening Prayer: A Blessing Over You**

**Father, in the name of Jesus**, I lift up the reader of this book before Your throne of grace. You see every storm, every test, every question, and every hidden tear. Thank You that nothing surprises You - and nothing is bigger than You.

Holy Spirit, breathe peace over this son/daughter right now. Remind them of truth: *"As He is, so are we in this world"* (1 John 4:17). The same Christ who rose in victory lives within them. Let that reality settle deep - into mind, heart, and soul.

Lord, shape their mindset for victory. Plant courage, unwavering faith, determination, and endurance. Where fear has spoken, let faith speak louder. Where weariness sits heavy, pour fresh strength. Where there is confusion, release clarity and wise strategy.

I declare over them: You will make it. You will get through this. You will reach the other side. And when the test is passed, promotion follows – because promotion comes from You.

Father, anchor them in identity. You made them in Your image and after Your likeness. You gave them a mind to think, hands to build, and a heart to persevere. Stir up holy creativity to solve problems and unlock solutions. Let them live from who they are - not helpless, but helped, not victims, but victors.

By the faith of Christ within them, let them move with Heaven's confidence and authority. I decree Your Word: you are the head and not tail, above only and not beneath (Deuteronomy 28:13); greater is He that is in you than he that is in the world (1 John 4:4); no weapon formed against you shall prosper (Isaiah 54:17).

Jesus, thank You that victory is not something we chase - it's the position we live from. You came that we might have life more abundantly (John 10:10). Lead this reader as a true child of God; let Your Spirit bear witness with their spirit that they are heirs of God and joint-heirs with Christ (Romans 8:14–17). Seat them in the awareness of their place with You in heavenly places (Ephesian 2:6).

Before they were formed in the womb, You knew them (Jerimiah 1:5). You knew this season, this challenge, this exact page – and You prepared grace for it. Now, in Jesus' name, I call forth elevation, strengthening, and forward movement. Open doors no one can shut. Close doors that don't belong to them. Surround them with favor like a shield.

Bless their soul to prosper, mind clear, heart whole, and emotions steady. Bless their body with health and recovery. Bless their work with insight and increase. Bless their relationships with unity and joy. And bless the journey ahead as they read: let this book be a key, a confirmation, and a new beginning that thrust them into their destiny.

Finally, I declare and decree that they are God's *Beloved, and I wish above all things that you prosper and be in health, even as your soul prospers* (3 John 2).

**I seal this prayer in the mighty name of Jesus.**
**Amen**

**Making It Happen:** The Shift from Inspiration to Implementation

I have a theory.
Most people attend a class, seminar, or even a church service looking for a spark of inspiration, or something to make them feel motivated, hopeful, and energized.

But here's the truth I've learned over decades in business, ministry, and life: **Inspiration without implementation is just emotional entertainment**.

It might move your emotions, but it won't move your life forward.

II Kings 4:1–7 paints this picture perfectly.
The servant of the Lord feared and reverenced God, but when he died, he left his wife in debt. The creditors were coming to take her sons as slaves to pay what he owed.

This widow didn't just cry and hope for sympathy. She called on the prophet Elisha - not just for a prayer, but for a strategy.

**And Elisha gave her one:**

"Go, borrow vessels, fill them with oil, and sell it to pay the debt."

She didn't hold a committee meeting.
She didn't wait until the conditions were perfect.
She didn't go back to bed and "think about it."

Scripture says she left immediately and began implementing the plan.

**The miracle was in her movement**.

---

**Breaking Down the Strategy**

Go

Elisha's first instruction was one word: "Go."
Not "wait," not "see how things play out," but move.

Faith has feet. The blessing didn't come while she stood still; it came when she stepped out.

---

**Borrow Vessels**

Elisha's next command was very specific: borrow vessels – and not a few.

**Why borrow instead of buy?**

- Time was critical – buying would have delayed the miracle.
- She had to activate relationships – knocking on doors, explaining her need, involving her community in the miracle.
- Capacity determined the outcome – the more vessels she borrowed, the more room there was for God to fill.

She sent her sons running through the neighborhood, collecting every empty container they could find.

**Here's the key principle:** the flow of blessing always stops where your preparation ends.

If they had gathered 10 jars, that's all God would have filled.
If they gathered 1000, the oil would have flowed into all 1000.

---

**Fill the Vessels**

Back at home, she started pouring her small amount of oil.
This is where faith looks foolish – because the miracle didn't happen before she poured.
**It happened as she poured**.

Every vessel filled to the brim.
And the oil only stopped when they ran out of containers.

---

### Sell It and Pay the Debt

Elisha told her to sell the oil and pay the debt - not go shopping, not splurge, and not waste the increase.

She was to become a producer, not just a consumer.
She took the proceeds, paid her debts, and she and her children lived on the rest **(that's generational wealth)**. *It worked for her, it has worked for me, and* ***it will work for you too***.

That's what obedience looks like.
That's what Kingdom stewardship looks like.

---

### Bringing It Closer to Home

**Now**, let's talk about you.

How many books have you read in the last five years on investing, money management, or building wealth?
How many podcasts, YouTube videos or training courses have you consumed?

**Here's the harder question – how much of it have you acted on?**

- Have you gone driving for dollars?
- Started tracking your spending to see where the leaks are?
- Taken steps to improve your credit?
- Purchased an asset that puts money in your pocket instead of taking it out?

The widow didn't just collect information – she collected oil.

**And oil only flowed when she followed the instructions**.

The same is true for you.
You don't need more "someday" dreams; **you need strategies you can start moving on today**.

---

**From the Widow's House to Your House**

This chapter – Faith *& Mindset: The Bedrock of the "Wealth Code" Unlocked* – is not written to inspire you for an afternoon.
It's here to give you the keys, the blueprint, and the boldness to start moving in actionable faith - because **miracles still happen, but they meet you in motion**.

And now that you've seen what faith in action looks like, let's take a step back and take a deeper look at **"Now Faith".**

---

**"Now faith is the substance of things hoped for, the evidence of things not seen." – Hebrews 11:1 (KJV)**

I want you to pause for a moment.
Don't rush past that verse like it's just another line in the Bible.

Let it breathe in your spirit.
Close your eyes and picture it.

Faith is not wishful thinking. It's not the same as a daydream or a positive vibe. **Faith is substance** – something you can spiritually stand on, lean on, and build on before it shows up in your bank account, your deed book, your body, or your business revenue.

When the writer of Hebrews said "substance," he was saying faith has weight, mass, and structure. It's like the steel beams inside a skyscraper - you may not see them from the street, but they're holding the whole thing together. Without them, the building collapses. Without faith, your dream collapses.

And faith is **evidence** – the legal proof in Heaven's court that what God promised is already yours. In our justice system, a lawyer doesn't win a case based on emotions; they win by presenting evidence. Evidence doesn't predict a win - it *secures* it. In the Kingdom, faith is the documented, signed, sealed, and notarized proof that what you're believing for has already been decided in your favor.

That's why Hebrews doesn't say, "Tomorrow faith" or "Someday faith." It says **NOW faith** - because faith is not a thing you file-away for later when conditions are perfect. Faith must be active in the moment. It reaches into the unseen realm, grabs hold of what God promised and by faith pull it into the visible realm.

I've lived this. I've walked into boardrooms, seller offices, and bank meetings with nothing in my natural hand but everything in my spiritual hand. Deals that looked impossible still closed – not because of my bank balance, but because my faith balance was strong enough to transact business in Heaven's economy.

**Let me tell you something** – you don't have to wait for the evidence to appear before you act. **Faith itself is your evidence.** The title deed exists in the spirit long before it gets printed at the courthouse.

So, **the real question is:** Are you waiting to "see" before you move, or are you willing to move so you can see **"The Inner Vault"**?

---

**The Inner Vault – Where Wealth Really Begins**

Most people, when they hear "wealth", imagine a vault, an inheritance, a big check, or some once-in-a-lifetime opportunity.
But here's the reality: **Wealth doesn't start in your wallet – it starts in your mind.**

I can teach you every proven technique for building wealth.
I can hand you the exact strategies I've used in real estate to acquire properties, grow cash flow, and multiply assets. I can give you the scripts, the formulas, the checklists, and the blueprints.

**But here's the hard truth** – if ***you never make the shift in your mindset, nothing will change for long***.

You might see a quick win here or there, but without a transformed mindset, old habits will creep back in. You'll sabotage your progress without even realizing it. You'll talk yourself out of deals you should step into. You'll shrink back when you should lean forward.

Because **wealth isn't built on techniques alone – it's sustained by the way you think, believe, and act**.

**Mindset is the difference** between making a little money once and **creating generational wealth that lasts**. It's the foundation under everything else. Without it, all the tactics in the world are like building a mansion on sand.

---

**What's the Purpose of Money? (Mindset Check)**

Before we dive into strategies and tactics, let me ask you a question: ***What do you really believe money is for (what's the purpose)?***

You don't have to answer out loud – your **daily habits already tell the truth louder than your words**. To make it plain, let me share a simple story.

**Three neighbors. Three paychecks. Three mindsets.**

**The Poor Family (Survival Mode)**
The paycheck hits the bank at 9:17 a.m. By lunchtime, it's already gone – rent, car note, utilities, groceries, late fees. Whatever's left might cover dinner. For them, **money's purpose is survival: pay today's bills and keep the lights on**. There's effort, hustle, and heart – but no margin. Money shows up and immediately disappears into someone else's pocket… **building someone else's assets**.

**The Middle Family (Comfort/Credit Mode)**
The paycheck comes in. Auto-pay takes care of the SUV loan, the furniture-store promo, and two credit cards. Reward points feel like small victories. Retirement contributions go into the 401(k), and a little goes to savings. **The purpose of money here is stability: build good credit, buy more things, pay them off over time, and set aside for retirement**. It's comfortable – but it's costly, because most purchases lose value the moment they're made.

**The Wealthy Family (Owner/Investor Mode)**
The paychecks arrive, but the first move isn't bills – it's investments. Fifteen percent goes into an index fund, another slice into a business account. Rental income pays for the car. A cash-flowing property and compounding investments quietly go to work in the background. For them, **money's purpose is multiplication: turning money into more money**. Assets get paid first, and those assets generate more assets. **Their money is making "babies" – and those babies grow up to make even more babies**. That's the cycle of wealth. **Note:** ***For the most part – they're the ones signing the front of the check, not the back***.

**Here's the key:** none of these mindsets define who you are – they're just patterns. And the good news? **Patterns can be changed.**

**Remember what Proverbs 23:7** (KJV) says: ***"For as he thinketh in his heart, so is he."*** Your inner beliefs shape your outer reality – money included. If your **thoughts are stuck in scarcity**, your actions will reflect that lack, and so will your bank account.

**But when your thinking shifts from survival to stewardship, from consumption to ownership, everything changes.** Your habits start to align differently – you invest, you build, you multiply. **That's why building true wealth isn't just about having money – it's** ***about how you think, and how the right mindset makes your money move with purpose.***

**When my mindset shifted, something inside me came alive**. I wanted to **learn the tools and skillsets** that could change the trajectory of my life – and not just mine, but also the lives of my family and friends.

**Real estate and investments became those tools for me**. And if I could learn them, use them, and grow from them, you can too.

**Never forget:** ***the story you believe about money will ultimately determine the story money tells about you.***

---

**The Purpose of Money (Mindset Patterns)**

| **Mindset** | **Daily Pattern** | **Purpose of Money** | **Result** |
|---|---|---|---|
| **Poor Family (Survival Mode)** | Paycheck gone by noon– rent, car, utilities, groceries, late fees. Dinner covered if anything is left. | Pay today's bills and keep the lights on. | **Hustle without margin. Money flows out to build someone else's assets.** |
| **Middle Family (Comfort/Credit Mode)** | Auto-pay hits: SUV note, furniture promo, credit cards. Earn rewards, contribute to 401(k), save for retirement. | Build credit, buy things, pay them off over time, and save for later. | **Comfortable but costly. Most purchases lose value while debt lingers.** |
| **Wealthy Family (Owner/Investor Mode)** | First move: invest– 15% to index funds, a slice to business. Rental income covers car. Assets grow quietly in the background. | Turn money into more money– multiplication and ownership. | **Assets pay bills, then create more assets. Money makes money (and keeps multiplying).** |

**Simple definitions:**
**Asset** = puts money in your pocket.
**Liability** = takes money out of your pocket.
**Goal = let income-producing assets make money *(and money babies)* that pay for your liabilities and grow into generational wealth**.

**Quick upgrades (wherever you are)**

- **One decision:** Set an automatic transfer to an investment or asset account the moment income hits. Start small, raise it quarterly.
- **One constraint:** No new debt for things that don't pay you. If you finance it, make sure it feeds you.
- **One skill:** Learn a money skill that compounds (budgeting, analyzing a rental, basic index investing).
- **One lens:** Before any purchase, ask: *Does this put money in my pocket – or take it out?*

You're not stuck in a category. **You're building a new pattern** – one **automatic move at a time**.

---

**Kingdom Finances (Mindset)**

**Narrative: Three Money Mindsets**

Most of us were trained to think about money in one of three ways. **The first is survival** – the **Poor Mindset**. Here, money's main job is to catch bills before they catch you. Cash comes in and rushes right back out to rent, food, and fees. Credit isn't a tool; it's a trap. When life hits, government programs or family help often fill the gap. It's hard to build wealth when you're always bailing water (robbing Brother Bill Peter - to pay Brother Bill Paul).

**Next is the security lane** – the **Middle-Class Mindset**. This path prizes education, a good job, and a solid credit score. You buy the house, contribute to savings and a 401K/403b retirement plan, maybe pick a few mutual funds or a small rental. It feels stable, and it is - yet the focus is still mainly on income from your labor and paying debts. You're making more and-more money, to buy more and more stuff." You are comfortable here and you enjoy looking at that bank account with $100K - $500K, and even a $million in it for some of you – and you are thrilled and excited (as you should be for this accomplishment). **However, think about this:**

Here's a comparison of the purchasing power of **$100,000 today versus $100,000 three years ago parked in your bank**:

---

**How Much Has $100,000 Lost in Purchasing Power?**

- **Cumulative inflation from 2022 to 2025** is approximately **10.38%**, based on Consumer Price Index (CPI) data. in2013dollars.com
- That means: **$100,000 in 2022** would purchase what now costs about **$110,380** today.

**In other words:**

- **$100,000 today** has the same buying power as around **$90,700** did in 2022.
- You've lost approximately **$9,300** in real purchasing power.

---

**Summary Table**

| Year | CPI Increase | Real Equivalent of $100,000 Today |
|---|---|---|
| 2022 | – | $100,000 |
| 2025 | +10.38% | **$90,710** |

---

**Key Insight**

**What felt like a winning $100K balance back in 2022 doesn't stretch as far today**. That cushion has been **chipped away by inflation over just three years** – even though headline rates of 2–3% may seem modest, compounding shifts change the real picture significantly.

**Let's go deeper (check this out):**

Here's how inflation erosion looks when you scale it up for $100K, $500K, and $1M sitting in the bank untouched over the past 3 years (2022 → 2025):

**Assumption:**

- **Cumulative inflation (2022–2025): ~10.38%**
  (Source: U.S. Bureau of Labor Statistics CPI data)

---

**Purchasing Power Today (vs. 2022)**

| Nominal Bank Balance | Real Value Today (Adjusted for Inflation) | Lost Purchasing Power |
|---|---|---|
| **$100,000** | ≈ **$90,700** | –$9,300 |
| **$500,000** | ≈ **$453,500** | –$46,500 |
| **$1,000,000** | ≈ **$907,000** | –$93,000 |

---

**What It Means**

- Three years ago, **$100K could buy what now costs $110,380.**
- Keeping $500K or $1M "safe" in the bank without outpacing inflation eroded **tens of thousands** in real value.
- In effect, inflation acts like a **silent tax** – especially on idle cash balances.

**Let's project this forward 10 years** (e.g., if inflation averages 3–4% annually), showing the *future cost* of parking money in the bank?

Inflation Impact Over 10 Years

| **Nominal Bank Balance (Today)** | **Real Value in 10 Years (Adjusted for 3.5% Inflation)** | **Lost Purchasing Power** |
|---|---|---|
| $100,000 | $70,892 | -$29,108 |
| $500,000 | $354,459 | -$145,541 |
| $1,000,000 | $708,919 | -$291,081 |

The table shows how $100K, $500K, and $1M sitting in the bank would erode in **real value over 10 years** if inflation averages just **3.5% per year**.

**Can you see how much purchasing power disappears even though the bank balance number looks the same?**

***The Ownership Lane – The Wealth Mindset**

**In the ownership lane, money's assignment is multiplication.** Dollars are not trophies to be admired – they are employees that need jobs. **The goal here is not just to earn income, but to deploy income into assets that pay you back: businesses, real estate investments, and other vehicles designed to multiply wealth.** The wealthy study money on purpose, learn the tools, and then buy or build cash-flowing assets that support their lifestyle *and* their giving.

---

**How the Wealthy Think (vs. Middle-Class Thinking)**

- **Middle-Class Mindset:** "Save money in the bank, keep a good credit score, buy more stuff over time, and pay off debt slowly."

- **Wealth Mindset:** "Stage money in the bank briefly for transactions and emergencies, then deploy it into assets that grow, generate cash flow, and create tax advantages."

**Key difference: For the wealthy, banks are a parking lot for short-term use, not a warehouse where money sits idle and loses value to inflation.**

---

**The Wealth Operating System**

**Think of it as five steps:**

1. Earned income flows into asset accounts first (before expenses).
2. Deploy capital into cash-flowing assets (rental properties, small businesses, dividend-paying stocks, etc.).
3. Reinvest the cash flow (instead of spending it all).
4. Use tax levers like depreciation (paper deductions from real estate), 1031 exchanges (a tax-deferred swap of one property for another), or Qualified Business Income (QBI) deductions to keep more money working.
5. Protect and repeat using entities (LLCs for limited liability protection), insurance, and reserves.

---

**This is why Jesus didn't just perform miracles – He often challenged the way people thought. He knew that until your thinking changes, your results can't change.**

Before you ever acquire property, raise capital, close a deal, or hold the keys to your first investment, you must settle one thing deep within your heart:

**What do you believe about yourself, your future, and your God-given purpose?**

Here's **the truth** – "**Mindset is the Gatekeeper of Manifestation**". It's the soil where ideas are planted, decisions are formed, and **wealth is either birthed or blocked**.

If your mindset is saturated with doubt, fear, lack, or outdated programming, even a million-dollar opportunity will look like a threat.
But when your mindset is rooted in faith, clarity, and Kingdom truth, you'll begin to **see what others cannot, do what others won't**, and **build what others said was impossible**.

---

**Mindset Inventory – Quick Self-Check**

Before we move forward, take a moment to rate yourself from 1–10

(1 = weak, 10 = strong):

- I believe God wants me to prosper. ___
- I can clearly see my role in advancing His Kingdom. ___
- I make decisions from faith, not fear. ___
- I take consistent action toward my wealth-building goals. ___
- I believe I can and will leave a legacy that outlives me. ___

If any score is **less than 8**, mark it. Those are the areas we will strengthen as we unlock your **"Wealth Code"**.

---

**Back to the Blueprint**

**"And God said, Let us make man in our image, after our likeness: and let them have dominion…"** – ***Genesis 1:26 (KJV)***

This is not poetic language.
This is your **original blueprint**.

**You were created in the image and likeness of God – designed to:**

- **Think creatively**
- **Speak authoritatively**
- **Build strategically**
- **Govern responsibly**

**Dominion is in your DNA.**
You weren't created to beg, borrow just to survive, or settle for crumbs. You were created to build, to own, to multiply, and to advance God's purposes in the earth.

---

**Pause and Picture This**

Imagine Adam's first moments on earth – breathing in the oxygen God had just spoken into existence, standing in a garden he didn't plant but was given to manage.
God hands him the title deed to Eden without a down payment, without a credit check, without an inspection report.

That's Kingdom wealth – not just owning, but **stewarding** what God entrusts you with, so it multiplies.

---

**The Systems That Trained You to Settle**

Now here's the reality – most **of us weren't raised to think like Kingdom Advancers**.

**We were shaped by systems** – educational, cultural, financial, and sometimes even religious – that conditioned us to survive, not to reign.

We were told things like:

- "Money doesn't grow on trees."
- "Stay in your lane."
- "Play it safe."
- "Don't dream too big."
- "Wealth is for them, not you."
- "A rich man or woman cannot enter the Kingdom"

And here's one of **the most dangerous lies** ever spoken in church culture: **"Poverty equals holiness."**

That's not Kingdom thinking – that's **programming**. And programming can be rewritten. But first, you must **recognize it for what it is**.

---

### Trading Security for Dominion – When "Playing It Safe" Misses God's Heart

It was 1984, and I had been out of the Air Force for nearly two decades. My first civilian job after active duty paid $4.35 an hour – a humble start for someone who had served eight years. **Fast forward twenty years**, and life looked very different.

I was now serving as an Associate Director (Small Business Office) for a high-level technical procurement information systems program in the U.S. Army. It was a government position with prestige, a six-figure salary, great benefits, and a 401K. By every measure, it was the kind of job people dream about retiring from.

One afternoon, I shared a dream with a co-worker – a dream that had been quietly growing in my heart.

**"I want to own my own business," I said. "And I want to invest in property."**

She chuckled softly, shaking her head. "How are you going to leave this good government job with all these benefits?"

Her tone wasn't cruel – in fact, she meant well. She wanted to protect me from risk, from failure, from what she thought might be disappointment. But in trying to protect me from failure… she was unknowingly trying to protect me from faith.

**If I had listened to her, you wouldn't be reading this book right now. There would be no real estate portfolio. No coaching students. No "Wealth Code" Unlocked to pass on. I would have traded dominion for security… and missed my assignment entirely**.

I knew walking away wasn't just a career move – it was an act of obedience. I was stepping out of a comfort zone that many people spend their entire careers trying to get into. But something deep inside told me this was the time. God was leading me into the next chapter: working for myself in real estate, both as an investor and as a commercial real estate agent.

**Let's be clear** – it wasn't easy. Faith rarely is. It took courage to voluntarily leave behind a stable paycheck, incredible benefits, and a secure retirement plan simply because I felt led to do so. But I can tell you this – the same God who sustained me when I depended on free Olympic meal tickets back in the 1980s was the same God orchestrating this leap of faith.

He provided. He guided. He opened doors I could not have forced open myself. And I learned something that has never left me: His favor and provision are not bound by a season, a salary, or a benefits package. They follow those who trust Him – in times of scarcity and in seasons of abundance, in humble beginnings and in bold new ventures.

**The truth is**, if your mindset is locked on "security," you'll miss opportunities that require "**faith**." And **in the Kingdom, the real wealth – the kind that impacts generations – is always on the other side of obedience**.

---

**Practical Key – How to Break Old Programming**

1. Identify the limiting belief. ("Money is evil," "I'm not good with numbers," "Success isn't for people like me.")
2. Replace it with a Kingdom truth. ("The love of money is the root of evil – money **is a tool in the hands of the righteous**.")
3. Speak the truth daily until your mind believes it more than the lie.
4. Take one small action that proves the truth is real.

**The Wealth Assignment**

**"But thou shalt remember the Lord thy God: for *it is he that giveth thee power to get wealth*, that he may establish his covenant** which he sware unto thy fathers, as it is this day." – Deuteronomy 8:18 (KJV)

**"A good man leaveth an inheritance to his children's children: and the wealth of the sinner is laid up for the just."** – Proverbs 13:22 (KJV)

These verses don't just talk about financial gain.
They point to a **multi-generational assignment** – an unbroken chain of stewardship, covenant, and Kingdom expansion.

One generation builds the foundation.
The next generation builds higher.
And your children's children walk on floors they didn't have to lay.

This is **wealth that outlives you**.

---

**Reflection Pause – Your Assignment**

Before you go any further, write this down:

**1. What's your plan to build and advance the work of the Kingdom in your sphere of influence?**

✎ ______________________________________________

✎ ______________________________________________

✎ ______________________________________________

**2. What's your strategy to leave a legacy and an inheritance for your children's children (those beautiful grandbabies)?**

✎ ______________________________________________

✎ ______________________________________________

✎ ______________________________________________

---

**When Real Faith Met Real Racism**

In Virginia, I discovered a subdivision with a dark past.
One of its deeds, dated **April 6, 1948, read:**

"**These lots shall not**, within a period of 100 years… **be conveyed, sold, leased to, owned, or occupied by any negro**…"

This wasn't ancient history – this was **post-WWII America.**
And the author of that document? The **Commonwealth's Attorney** of a rural Virginia county.
His son later became a judge.

These weren't random bigots – these were **gatekeepers of justice**, legally scripting out exclusion and generational denial.

---

**The Day the Paper Burned in My Hands**

I stood there with the photocopy of the deed in my hands, the paper yellowed by time but still bold with ink that dripped with arrogance.
The words didn't just jump off the page – they **burned**.
They carried the weight of decades of **closed doors**, **denied dreams**, and **stolen opportunities**.

I thought about the families who drove by that neighborhood, knowing without being told, ***"This isn't for you."***
I thought about the young man who might have wanted to buy a home there to raise his family but was **legally forbidden** – not because of his finances, his character, or his ability to pay, but because of the melanin in his skin.

---

This was more than ink on paper.
This was a **blueprint for generational theft** – a script written by those in power to ensure that wealth and opportunity stayed locked away from people who looked like me.

And yet, as I stared at those words, I felt two things at once:
**Deep anger**… and a **strange sense of destiny (I had a choice)**.

That's when my Father spoke something that shifted everything:

**"You're not here to protest. You're here to possess."**

---

**From Anger to Assignment**

I knew exactly what He meant.
My assignment wasn't to stand outside the gates shouting – it **was to walk through the gates and take ownership**.

**Now check God out** – He used an elderly gentleman who didn't look like me – Mr. **David Jefferson** (name changed) – to finance over **100%** of the purchase.

**When the deal closed *(I had my own rally)* I marched away with *the* keys; I marched away with *the* deed; and I marched away with *a* check (*run that play*).**

That's not just **favor**.
**That's Now Faith**.
That's what it means to **walk (or march)** in the "**Wealth Code"** – to **own** what was once denied, to **stand** where others said you don't belong, and to **receive** what no one thought you could have. **"Wealth Code" Unlocked**.

---

**Practical Key – Turning Injustice into Inheritance**

1. Identify a closed door in your industry or community.
2. Research the barriers – are they legal, financial, relational, or cultural?
3. Ask God for strategy, not just sympathy.
4. Partner with people who have access you don't.
5. Take possession – legally, ethically, and unapologetically.

**How Divine Favor Met Daily Needs in Unexpected Ways**

When I look back over my life, I can see the unmistakable fingerprints of God – weaving **favor** into ordinary and extraordinary moments, especially during times of uncertainty.

Some of those seasons looked impossible on paper…
But the **"Wealth Code" Unlocked** isn't just about having millions in the bank – it's about **knowing Who your Source** is, no matter the season.

---

**Life After the Air Force – A Hard Landing**

After serving **eight years of active duty** in the United States Air Force and achieving the rank of **Staff Sergeant (E5)**, I transitioned out with a plan:

- Go to college.
- Join the Air National Guard.
- Rely on unemployment benefits while I made my next steps.

I'd been working part-time since age 13 and full-time since the 11th grade, so when I suddenly found myself at home – idle – I lasted three weeks before restlessness pushed me back into the workforce.

I landed my first civilian job as an electronics assembler at Metric Systems in Fort Walton Beach, Florida.
The pay? **$4.35 an hour**.
A modest sum for someone with military leadership and technical training.

---

**The Math Didn't Add Up**

To give perspective: I already owned a home, and my mortgage was about **$535 a month**.
My part-time shifts in the Air National Guard weren't enough, and I wasn't eligible for unemployment benefits.

The math was simple:
More money going out than coming in.
And I was running out of options.

---

**From Military Meal Cards to McDonald's Miracles**

In the military, a **meal card** meant guaranteed food.
No matter what, the chow hall was there.
But as a civilian, those comforts were gone.

It was 1984, and the Summer Olympics were approaching.
The USSR had just announced a boycott – a major blow to the Games but an unexpected setup for me.

**Why?** Because McDonald's launched a promotion:

- US Gold medal = free Big Mac
- US Silver medal = free fries
- US Bronze medal = free Coke

---

### An Unlikely Connection

At the time, I was friends with a young woman who worked at McDonald's. In an act of quiet generosity, she handed me a **stack** of those Olympic giveaway tickets.

With the USSR out of competition, the U.S. began **dominating** event after event. Gold after gold. Silver after silver. Bronze after bronze. Almost every ticket I had turned into a **winner**.

### God's Provision in the Ordinary

Hungry and unsure how I'd afford my next meal, I walked into McDonald's with my stack of winning tickets.
Big Macs. Fries. Cokes.
More food than I could have imagined at a time when I needed it most.

God had used something as **global** as an Olympic boycott and as **ordinary** as a fast-food promotion to make sure His son had enough to eat.

---

### Practical Key – Recognizing Hidden Provision

1. Don't overlook small or unconventional blessings.
2. Keep your pride in check – provision often comes in unexpected packages.

3. Stay faithful in tithing and giving, even in lean seasons.
4. Remember: your source is God, not your paycheck.

**Declaration**:
*"I am never without provision. My Father knows my needs before I ask, and He always makes a way."*

---

### The 4 Keys of the "Wealth Code" Unlocked – Expanded

The "Wealth Code" isn't a mystery.
It's a set of **spiritual and practical keys** that, when applied, unlock both opportunity and destiny.
I've lived them – in the military, in real estate, in business, and in lean seasons where I had to trust God for my next meal.

---

### Key 1: You Have What God Says You Have

You're not lacking – you're loaded.
God has already placed inside you **everything you need** by His Spirit.

**Scriptural Truths**:

- You are made in His image – Genesis 1:26
- You have the mind of Christ – 1 Corinthians 2:16
- You are more than a conqueror – Romans 8:37
- Greater is He that is in you – 1 John 4:4
- You are the head, not the tail – Deuteronomy 28:13
- All your needs are met – Philippians 4:19

**Checklist for Key 1**:

☑ Identify 3 areas where you've been saying "I don't have enough."

☑ Replace those statements with declarations of abundance.

☑ List current skills, assets, and connections you already have that can be leveraged now.

**Declaration**:
*"I am equipped. I am resourced. I am lacking nothing in Christ. Everything I need to fulfill my Kingdom assignment is already in my possession."*

**Key 2: You Are Not Alone in the Storm**

In Mark 6, Jesus told His disciples to get into the boat and go to the other side.
He knew the storm would come.
And when it did, He walked on the very water that threatened them.

Peter didn't walk on water because it was calm – he walked because the **invitation was divine**.

---

**The Lesson in the Storm**

Storms are not signs that you missed God.
They are often **confirmation** that you're on assignment.

If your journey is Kingdom-focused, you'll face resistance – spiritual, mental, financial, and relational.
The enemy doesn't waste energy fighting people who aren't a threat.

---

**Practical Checklist for Key 2**:

☑ When storms hit, ask: "Am I on the path God told me to take?"

☑ Speak the promise louder than the problem.

☑ Keep moving – storms are temporary.

**Declaration**:
*"God is with me in every storm. I will not fear the waves; I will walk on them."*

---

## Key 3: Faith Is for the Fight, Not Just the Finish Line

We love the idea of "mountain-moving faith," but often forget that mountains must first be **climbed** before they can be conquered.

The woman with the issue of blood didn't wait for a perfect moment – she **pressed** through the crowd, risking shame and rejection. She declared her healing before she saw it.

---

### Faith That Presses

Faith isn't just for celebrating the breakthrough – it's for pushing toward it. This kind of faith requires endurance.

---

**Practical Checklist for Key 3**:

☑ Identify one area you've been waiting for "perfect conditions."

☑ Take one action step toward it today.

☑ Write down your declaration of victory before you see it.

**Declaration**:
*"I will not quit. I will press until my breakthrough comes. I will not be denied."*

---

### Key 4: You Can Do All Things Through Christ

You are a **Kingdom ambassador** with supernatural backing.
The Holy Spirit empowers you to:

- Create wealth.
- Break generational curses.
- Build businesses.
- Acquire property.
- Leave a lasting legacy.

---

**Practical Checklist for Key 4**:
☑ Dream without limits – list 10 things you'd do if you knew you couldn't fail.
☑ Identify 3 that align most with your Kingdom assignment.
☑ Start mapping the first step for each.

**Declaration**:
*"I can do all things through Christ. No vision is too big. No assignment is impossible. I am unstoppable with God."*

---

**The Daily Builder's Routine – Activating the "Wealth Code" Unlocked works the same way.**
It's not something you **memorize** – it's something you **live daily**.

---

### 1. Daily Declarations – Frame Your Day Before It Frames You

Speak God's truth over your life before you let the world speak over you.

"Thou shalt also decree a thing, and it shall be established unto thee" (Job 22:28).

**Example Declarations:**

- "I am a wise steward of all God entrusts to me."
- "Opportunities find me, and I am prepared to receive them."
- "The favor of God surrounds me like a shield."

---

**2. Scripture Meditation – Let the Word Rewire You**

A renewed mind doesn't happen by accident.

"But his delight is in the law of the Lord; and in his law doth he meditate day and night" (Psalm 1:2).

**Example Practice:**

- Read (Deuteronomy 8:18) and ask: "Father, what does **'power to get wealth'** look like for me today?"
- Journal any strategies or impressions you receive.

---

**3. Environment Check – Surround Yourself with Builders**

"He that walketh with wise men shall be wise: but a companion of fools shall be destroyed" (Proverbs 13:20).

**Example Practice:**

- Limit time with people who drain or distract you.
- Seek out rooms where your vision feels small – and then grow into it.

---

**4. Information Diet – Feed What You Want to Grow**

"Keep thy heart with all diligence; for out of it are the issues of life" (Proverbs 4:23).

**Example Practice:**

- Replace 30 minutes of scrolling with 30 minutes of growth content.
- Curate what you watch, listen to, and read to align with Kingdom thinking.

---

**5. Faith in Action – Move Even When It's Messy**

"If ye be willing and obedient, ye shall eat the good of the land" *(Isaiah 1:19 KJV)*.

**Example Practice:**

- Make the call.
- Walk the property.
- Submit the proposal.
- Start before you "feel ready."

---

**Reflection & Notes to Self**

**Today, I will declare:**

---

---

**Today, I will meditate on:**

---

**Today, I will adjust my environment by:**

**Today, I will feed my mind with:**

**Today, I will take action by:**

**Reflection Questions – Building and Advancing the Kingdom**

1. What's your plan to build and advance the work of the Kingdom in your sphere of influence?

2. What's your strategy to leave a legacy and an inheritance for your children's children (those beautiful grandbabies)?

**The Silent Sin No One Talks About**

**We rarely hear it preached**, but **overspending and financial mismanagement are spiritual issues**.
Not because God is trying to condemn us – but because **poor stewardship is a breach of trust**. It's taking what He placed in our hands and failing to align it with His purposes.

When we fail to call **poor stewardship** what it is, there's no need to **repent**. And if there's **no repentance, there's no transformation**.
We keep cycling through the same frustrations, saying:

- "I'll do better next month."
- "If I had more money, I'd manage it better."
- "I'm just not good with numbers."

But the **Parable of the Talents** (Matthew 25:14–30) pulls back the curtain on God's perspective.
He doesn't just hand out resources; He expects **multiplication**.
He expects **accountability**.
And He rewards faithfulness while confronting fear, waste, and inaction.

**Until we see financial mismanagement as a Kingdom violation, we will keep sabotaging our own breakthroughs – praying for blessings we aren't prepared to manage**.

---

### The Financial Doctor's Orders

Just like a doctor gives you a prescription when your body is unhealthy, sometimes a pastor, mentor, coach or financial advisor gives you a prescription for your financial health:

- Build and follow a real budget.
- Stop overspending.
- Learn to manage money with wisdom.
- Expand your skills in investing, business, or real estate.
- Position yourself to multiply what you already have.

At first, these steps may feel restrictive – like a diet you don't want to be on – but they're actually pathways to **financial freedom**.

This is what **faith in action** looks like: aligning your daily behavior with your belief that God has called you to prosper and be a faithful steward.

---

### Why Stewardship Matters to the "Wealth Code" Unlocked

The **"Wealth Code" Unlocked** is not just about inspiration; **it's about transformation**.
It's the realization that God gives you **the power to get wealth** (Deuteronomy 8:18) – and with that power comes responsibility.

**Stewardship is the activator of every other principle you've learned**.
It's how you turn vision into action, belief into results, and potential into impact.

**When you manage what you have with wisdom:**

- You can fund Kingdom projects that change lives.
- You can create an inheritance for your children's children.
- You can live as a walking testimony that God's Word works.

Poor stewardship shuts those doors before you even get close to them. But disciplined, faithful stewardship throws them wide open.

---

### The Bridge to the Next Level

Faith gives you vision.
Mindset gives you direction.
But **stewardship** – the skillful management and multiplication of resources – turns both into reality.

This is the bridge between **hearing the promise** and **walking in the promise**.
The **"Wealth Code" Unlocked** calls you to move from theory into mastery – where every decision, every investment, and every act of generosity is on purpose and for purpose.

---

**Transition to Chapter 2**

In the next chapter, we're going to make the shift – moving from survival mode to thrive mode.
You'll learn how to take the keys you've just unlocked and start building a life that advances the Kingdom, impacts generations, and multiplies what's been placed in your hands.

Because the **"Wealth Code" Unlocked** is not something you just know – it's something you live.

**Let's shift gears…**

# Chapter 2

## **Thrive Mode:** Make the Shift

**From Position to Possession** – Living in Victory and Taking It by Force

Before you ever pick up a strategy, you must pick up your position.

**Victory in life, business, and wealth-building doesn't start with tactics – it starts with identity**. You don't fight for **victory; you fight from it**. That one shift changes everything.

If you don't know you're already positioned for victory, you'll approach challenges like a victim, not a victor. And victims play small, hesitate, and settle. **Victors take ground**.

---

### The Kingdom Position

(Ephesians 2:6) says:

"And hath raised us up together, and made us sit together in heavenly places in Christ Jesus."

That means you're not climbing to get favor – you're already seated in authority. The problem isn't with your spiritual position; it's with your mental posture.

**Operating from victory means:**

- You're not hustling to be accepted – you're building from being approved.
- You're not proving your worth – you're walking in your inheritance.
- You're not begging for a seat – you're expanding the table.

---

**Position Determines Perspective**

Where you sit determines what you see. And what you see determines how you move.

Think of an aerial drone view of a city. From the ground, traffic looks chaotic. But from above, patterns emerge. Routes become clear. Obstacles look smaller. Options appear.

That's the power of Kingdom positioning. From the seat of victory, you stop reacting in desperation and start moving with clarity and precision.

When you understand who you are and where you sit in Christ, you begin making faith-fueled moves, not fear-based ones.

---

**The "Take It By Force" Mindset**

Some opportunities in life will fall into your lap – but **most will not**.
The rest you will have to pursue with focus, discipline, and determination.

That's the "Take It By Force" mindset.

This isn't about aggression or hostility; it's about going after your God-given goals with intention, resilience, and an unshakable belief that you are built to win.

**It will require:**

- **Courage** – Stepping forward even when the outcome is uncertain.
- **Focus** – Blocking out distractions to stay locked on your target.
- **Resilience** – Bouncing back quickly when things don't go your way.
- **Endurance** – Pushing forward when it's difficult or uncomfortable.

---

## From Teaching to Testimony

Now, let me show you what this looks like in real life.

My real estate journey goes back to the days of Carlton Sheets – one of the original real estate educators teaching how to do no-money-down deals and even walk away from **closing with cash in hand**.

I remember signing up for his program, reading the material, and actually implementing it. At the time, we had moved from Alexandria, Virginia, to a more rural area that seemed to overflow with opportunity.

I kept studying and finally decided to test what I had learned.

---

## The Main Street Deal

I found a property on Main Street – two buildings on one parcel: a warehouse with an upstairs apartment and a thrift store next door.

I made an offer contingent on the seller agreeing to subdivide the property and hold a second mortgage.

The seller was asking $235,000. We agreed to $200,000, but here's the twist – we wrote the contract for $235,000 with $35,000 coming back to me at closing for improvements.

Then I asked for another $15,000 for a new roof. We settled on a $10,000 credit.

When the deal closed, I walked away with the deed, the keys… and a check for $36,000 in my pocket.

---

### The Flip Without Selling

About a year later (same deal from above), the restaurant owner next door wanted to buy the smaller parcel for extra parking. We settled on $190,000 – the same amount I had paid for both buildings. That meant the larger parcel – the warehouse – was now free and clear.

And it didn't stop there.

I had negotiated an option to demo the thrift store and salvage materials. Ten months later, I got paid another $10,000 not to demo.

---

### Turning Vision into Cash Flow

With a free and clear warehouse, I transformed it into a six-unit apartment building – three downstairs, two newly built upstairs, and the one that was already there.

That's not just investing. That's visionary investing. That's seeing what others missed.

**Ask yourself:** *How long would it take you to make – or save – **$200,000**?* This single deal created that and gave me a cash-flowing asset… all because I could see value that others couldn't see.

---

### It's Already in You

You have more capacity than you think. Every person has untapped potential – mental, emotional, creative – that gets activated when pressure and purpose collide.

No one is born ready for greatness. Readiness is forged in action. You develop it by moving forward, adapting to obstacles, and refusing to quit.

---

**Practical Keys to Walking in Victory**

1. Start Your Day in the Word – Remind yourself daily of your authority and assignment.
2. Pray from Authority – Declare what God has promised instead of begging for what's already yours.
3. Reject the Victim Mindset – Life doesn't just happen to you. You happen to life.
4. Protect Your Peace – Don't let outside chaos take residence inside you.
5. Surround Yourself with Builders – Stay in community with those who push you forward.

---

**The Thrive Mode Playbook – 7 Steps**

Thrive Mode is when faith and strategy merge. It's when you stop living on defense and start playing offense with your time, talent, and treasure. It's the mindset of no longer waiting for conditions to be perfect – you move forward with what you have, trusting God to multiply your steps.

**Here's your seven-step blueprint to shift from surviving to thriving:**

---

**1. Vision Alignment – Review** Your Goals Every Morning

Your vision is your compass. Without it, you drift. Every morning, take five minutes to read and speak your goals out loud. This isn't just about motivation – it's about alignment.
When you consistently see where you're going, your decisions naturally begin to match your destination. You'll find yourself asking:

***Does this action pull me closer to my vision, or push me further away?***

**Pro Tip:** Keep your goals in a visible place – on your bathroom mirror, phone lock screen, or journal – so you can't escape them.

**2. Opportunity Scanning – Look** for Ways to Advance Daily

Opportunities rarely knock; they hide in plain sight. Make it a daily habit to scan your environment for openings to grow, connect, or create value. This could be a conversation, a new skill, a partnership, or even a problem you can solve for profit.

**Pro Tip:** Train your mind to replace the question ***"Why not me?"*** with ***"Why not now?"***

---

**3. Action Over Analysis – Don't** Get Stuck in Planning Mode. **Move.**

Overthinking is a silent killer of dreams. Planning has its place, but too much of it is procrastination in disguise. Thrivers understand that imperfect action beats perfect inaction every time.
**You can course-correct in motion,** *but you can't steer a parked car.*

**Pro Tip: Set a 24-hour execution rule – if** you think of an idea or identify an opportunity, take at least one tangible action toward it within a day.

---

**4. Faith as Fuel – Let Belief Be the Engine for Every Decision**

Fear drains you! Faith fuels you! When your belief in God's promises becomes the engine for your decisions, you stop waiting for certainty and start moving on conviction.

Faith is not wishful thinking – it's acting on what God said before you see it. The more you move in faith, the more you'll see doors open that others didn't even know existed.

**Pro Tip:** Pair every major decision with a scripture that confirms it. Speak it until your spirit believes it.

---

**5. Set Stretch Goals – Pursue Targets That Require Growth**

If your goals don't make you a little nervous, they're too small. Stretch goals pull you out of your comfort zone, forcing you to think differently, manage differently, and lead differently.
The beauty of a stretch goal is that even if you fall short, you end up further than where you started.

**Pro Tip: Break big goals into "bite-sized battles" – small**, measurable wins that build momentum and confidence.

---

**6. Reframe Setbacks – See** Obstacles as Opportunities

**In Thrive Mode, setbacks are not stop signs – they are speed bumps that force** you to slow down, assess, and adjust. Every obstacle carries a lesson, a redirection, or a hidden advantage.

**Ask yourself:** *What is this situation here to teach me, prepare me for, or protect me from?*
That perspective keeps you in motion while others are stuck in frustration.

**Pro Tip:** Keep a "Setback Journal" where you record challenges and the lessons they brought. Over time, it will become a book of proof that you can overcome anything.

---

**7. Act Without Waiting for Permission – Leaders** Initiate

Thrivers don't wait for the "perfect time" or someone else's approval. They **move**. If God gave you the vision, **He already authorized the action. Waiting for permission can cost you years. Acting on your God-given assignment can produce results in weeks or months.**

**Pro Tip:** Treat every inspired idea as a divine assignment – start before you feel ready and let your preparation catch up to your action.

---

**Bottom line: The Thrive Mode Playbook** is not theory – it's a way of life. These seven steps, practiced daily, will rewire your mindset, sharpen your execution, and accelerate your results. And **the moment you combine this mindset with real estate strategies that work, your life will never be the same**.

## Thriving in Tough Times – God's Blueprint Still Works

### A Shaking World

Let's be honest. Times feel shaky right now. Prices at the store are still high. Some people are losing jobs. The news keeps talking about inflation, interest rates, trade wars, and whether the economy is slowing down or heating up. It's enough to make anyone nervous.

**But here's the truth:** God is not surprised by any of this. He knew these times were coming before we did. And He has already placed inside of us what we need not just to get through – but to come out stronger.

---

### Survival Is Not Enough

Most people are just trying to "hang on" until things get better. They're in survival mode: cutting back, worrying, waiting.

But Kingdom people - We're not called to *just survive.* We're called to thrive. Jesus didn't say, "I came so you could scrape by." He said, ***"I came that you might have life, and have it more abundantly"*** (John 10:10).

That means while the world panics, you can stand strong. While others pull back, you can press forward. **While some only see crisis, you can see opportunity**.

---

### God's System vs. Man's System

**The world's economic system** is built on fear and greed:

- Get all you can.
- Hold onto it.
- Look out for yourself.

**But God's system is the opposite**. His system is about **giving, trusting, and stewarding well** what He puts in your hand. And guess what? **His system works in *any* economy** – good or bad.

When others are shrinking back, the **Kingdom mindset says:**

- **"I will be faithful with what I have."**
- **"I will keep sowing."**
- **"I will listen for God's next instruction."**
- **"I will expect opportunities to come my way."**

---

### A Kingdom Example

Think about Joseph in the Bible. Life didn't treat him easy – thrown in a pit, sold as a slave, falsely accused, locked in prison. But **even in those hard places, he stayed faithful, and God positioned him for promotion**.

And when a famine hit, Joseph wasn't scrambling like everyone else. Why? Because he had listened to God's wisdom. He had a plan. He had storehouses ready. Instead of barely making it, he was feeding nations.

**That's the picture of thriving in hard times.**

---

### Practical Moves for Right Now

So what does **"thriving"** look like for you and me in today's economy? It's not about doing everything at once. It's about simple, steady steps:

1. **Pray and Listen Daily**
   Start your mornings asking, "Lord, what do You want me to see today?" He's always speaking.
2. **Stay Financially Ready**
   Don't overextend yourself. Build a little cushion. Cut what you don't need. Position yourself for opportunities.
3. **Look for Needs You Can Meet**
   Every crisis creates needs. People still need meals, services, encouragement, and solutions. Where can you serve?
4. **Be Open to New Ideas**
   Many new businesses are born in hard times. Ask God to show you the opportunities others are missing.
5. **Walk by Faith, Not Fear**
   Fear shrinks your vision. Faith enlarges it. Even if things look uncertain, God is bigger than the headlines.

---

### Speak This Over Your Life

**Say it out loud:**

- *I will survive this season – and **I will thrive**.*
- *I am not a victim of the economy. I am a child of the King.*
- ***I will see opportunities** where others see obstacles.*
- *I will be **faithful** with what I have, and **God will** multiply it.*

---

### The Other Side

Friend, **storms don't last forever** – but while they rage, God is not absent. In fact, **He blesses His people right in the middle of the storm**. The question is not just, *"Will I survive this season?"* but ***"How will God use this season to position me for what's next?"***

Joseph didn't just make it through prison; **he was promoted** through it. The very place that looked like defeat was the training ground for destiny. And the same God who was with Joseph is with you.

**When Covid-19 shut down the world, I stood before Lighthouse Marketplace Ministries and declared that we would not come out weaker, but stronger, wiser, and wealthier in every way that matters. And God proved Himself faithful**. Even while the storm raged, He was blessing His people – positioning us for what was on the other side. **From 2020 to 2022, real estate values increased year over year like nothing I had ever seen** in my 25 years of investing. While the headlines shouted fear, Heaven was writing a different story.

That's the nature of God. **He blesses in famine. He prospers in drought. He multiplies in crisis.** The storm doesn't stop His plan; it prepares you to carry it. And when the winds finally settle, you'll find that you haven't just endured – you've been equipped, elevated, and established for greater things.

The other side is not survival. It's strength. It's wisdom. It's wealth. It's testimony. And it starts right here, in the middle of the storm, where God is already at work in your favor. **Believe that, receive it, and walk in it NOW**.

**That's Kingdom economics. It works in every season. And it's yours to live out – starting now.**

**The Thrive Playbook**

**5 Bold Moves You Can Make Today**

1. **Pray for Direction**
   Take 10 quiet minutes to ask God, *"Show me where to move today."* Write down any ideas or nudges you sense.
2. **Check Your Finances**
   List your bills, income, and reserves. Pick one step to strengthen your position – cut one expense, add to savings, or pay down a small debt.

3. **Meet One Need**
   Look around: who can you encourage, serve, or bless today? Thriving starts by sowing into others.

4. **Spot One Opportunity**
   **Think:** what's in demand right now? Meals, online services, tutoring, delivery, coaching (look for a problem to solve)? Circle one idea that fits your skills.

5. **Speak Life**
   End your day declaring: *"I will thrive, not just survive.* ***My God is bigger than this season."***

---

**Simple, clear steps**. Not overwhelming – just daily choices that build momentum.

Victory is not something you chase – it's something you choose. You are already positioned for victory. You are equipped with authority, vision, and capacity. Now it's time to live like it – not passively waiting, but actively building, leading, and multiplying.

**Here's the key:** not all effort carries the same weight. **Some work gives you a paycheck, but other work creates freedom, influence, and legacy**. The difference comes down to the Kingdom level of value you operate in.

**The world will always pay you based on the Kingdom Level of Value you bring**. And the Kingdom of God has its own blueprint for how that value multiplies. **If you want to unlock true freedom, impact, and legacy, you must move into higher Kingdom Levels of Value.**

So **now**, let's go deeper. Let's **pull back the curtain on the framework** that explains why your labor has limits, why stewardship matters, why **your voice carries power, and why vision (Spirit-led vision) is the highest Kingdom level of all.**

# Chapter 3

## *The Kingdom Levels of Value*

***The Kingdom Levels of Value*** reveal a simple but profound truth: not all work produces the same return. Some efforts earn you a paycheck, others build influence, and the highest efforts create vision and legacy. As you rise through the levels – labor, management, influence, and Spirit-led vision – your impact multiplies.

I was first introduced to the idea of "levels of value" by my coach, Dr. Myron Golden. What you'll read here, however, is my own framework:

**The Kingdom Levels of Value** – is a faith-anchored, real estate-oriented application shaped by my definitions, labels, and examples.

**One of the greatest keys to unlocking the "Wealth Code" is learning how to shift into higher Kingdom Levels of Value**. When you understand which level you're operating in – and how to move higher – you stop trading hours for dollars and start aligning your value with purpose and stewardship. Scripture reminds us: ***"And whatsoever ye do, do it heartily, as to the Lord"*** (Colossians 3:23, KJV). **That's the mindset shift – from effort-driven income to purpose-directed value**.

Most people get stuck at the lowest Kingdom level – trading time for money. The problem is, there are only so many hours in a day you can physically work before your body starts to push back. Stress piles up, energy fades, and in time, your health begins to pay the price.

That's why you've got to **develop a plan** that takes you beyond just working for a paycheck. **Trading time for money can't be your only source of income**. *Learn to put systems, investments, and skillsets in place that allow your money to work even when you're not*. That's when you step out of survival mode and begin to operate at higher levels of Kingdom value – where multiplication, freedom, and legacy begin to take shape.

God has designed us for more: **In Genesis 1 and 2**, we see Him operating in multiple dimensions – **creating, speaking, blessing, assigning, and establishing order**. These are the very Kingdom Levels of value He has placed in us.

**Here's the underlying Truths and the Framework of The Kingdom Levels of Value:**

---

### Truth - The Resurrection Power of Christ in You

"But if the Spirit of Him that raised up Jesus from the dead dwell in you, He that raised up Christ from the dead shall also quicken your mortal bodies by His Spirit that dwelleth in you." (Romans 8:11)

### Why this chapter matters

This isn't theory. It's how you live, decide, and win – daily. If you belong to Jesus, the same Spirit that raised Him from the dead lives in you. That means you're built to operate with Kingdom Authority that fights through pressure, overcomes fear, and outmaneuvers the enemy.

### The Power Source Within

I often find myself closest to God when I'm near the water. It's something about the rhythm of the waves – steady, unhurried – that settles me. The sunlight shimmering and dancing across the surface of the water reminds me of His glory, while the sand beneath my feet grounds me in His creation. In that stillness, I can hear Him more clearly. My heart quiets, my spirit opens, and His presence feels undeniable.

It's in those sacred moments that I'm reminded of who I truly am: His workmanship, designed with intention, made in His very image. I don't just carry my own thoughts, burdens, or ideas – I carry His Spirit within me. That realization fills me with peace and strength, because I know I am never far from Him; His power flows through me.

When I'm by the water, I don't just see creation – I feel the Creator. And in His presence, I rediscover the source of everything I need: clarity, courage, wisdom, and rest.

**The Holy Spirit is not a vague idea. He is the power source that:**

- Illuminates the enemy's plans
- Strengthens your body, mind, and resolve
- Supplies wisdom on demand
- Moves you from inspiration to implementation

**Key thought: You're not trying to get power – you're learning to operate the power you already carry as Kingdom Sons and Daughters.**

---

**Don't Play with an enemy that's trying to kill you**

One night my wife and I watched an MMA pre-fight interview. One fighter said he just wanted to win. The other said something chilling: he wanted to destroy his opponent.

Sixty seconds into the fight, it was over. The man with the drive to destroy his opponent ended it quickly.

The next morning **the Lord dropped this on me:** That's how many believers approach warfare. The enemy isn't sparring with you - he's trying to steal, kill, and destroy you. Too often we "play nice," forgetting who lives in us. You have been given the power to destroy the enemy's (satan) plan over your life. You are more than a conqueror.

**Here's the good news:**

- Greater is He who is in you than he who is in the world (1 John. 4:4). **You have already won the fight**.
- **No weapon formed against you** shall prosper (Isaiah 54:17).

- You can do all things **through Christ who strengthens you** (Philippians 4:13).

This is not hype. **It's your covenant relationship** with the King.

---

**David's Pattern for Kingdom Level Living**

**Read (1 Samuel 17)** through this lens: David didn't face Goliath with boasting; he faced him knowing his covenant with God and the power of his testimony.

"The LORD who delivered me from the paw of the lion and the paw of the bear and He will deliver me from the hand of this Philistine." (1 Samuel 17:37)

**What David understood:**

- Covenant identity: He calls Goliath "an uncircumcised Philistine." Translation: no covenant.
- God's reputation: "You have defied the armies of the living God." (v.45)
- **Proven training:** The lion is dead. The bear is dead. Now this giant. Same God - new scale.

**David wasn't betting on his sling – he was tapping into his covenant with the Lord of Host and the Lord was with him.**

---

**How to Wage (and Win) Spiritual Warfare**

When the Holy Spirit lives in you, you don't fight for Victory – you fight from Victory.

**Four moves to make:**

1. **Speak to your situation**. Address it in the name of Jesus (Mark 11:23).

2. **Bind and Loose**. Shut down demonic activity and deception (Matthew 16:19).

3. **Decree and Declare**. Call forth God's peace, favor, and provision (Matthew 18:18–19).

4. Pray God's will on earth. **"Thy Kingdom come, Thy will be done…"** (Matthew 6:10).

**Prayer**
"In Jesus name, I bind every scheme of the enemy against my life, mind, and assignment. I loose the peace, wisdom, and favor of God. Father, let Your will be done here, now. Amen."

---

**When the Struggle Is Real**

**Some fights feel like lions and bears:** health battles, depression, compulsive habits, sexual immorality, manipulation and control, financial struggles, and substance abuse that won't let go.

God is not shocked. **He's on the throne**, and He is with you – to forgive, to deliver, to restore, and to realign you with your calling and purpose.

**Your next steps:**

1. **Confess and receive cleansing**. Pray (Psalms 51:10–12).

2. **Receive Jesus as Lord and Savior** (or re-dedicate your life to Him). Exchange your sin for His righteousness (2 Corinthians 5:21).

3. **Take the finished work personally**.

    - He bore your sickness: by His stripes **you are healed** (Isaiah 53:5).

- He took your poverty so you could **walk in provision** (2 Corinthians 8:9).

4. **Ask boldly**. Whatever you ask in My name, **that will I do** (John 14:13).

**The Promise: I know the plans I have for you… plans to prosper you and not to harm you… (Jeremiah 29:11)**

**Activation: Ask for Resurrection Power**

If you want it, ask for it – right now.

**Prayer of Activation**
"Lord Jesus, give me the **Resurrection Power of Christ** at work in me. Fill me afresh with the Holy Spirit.
Open my eyes to see, my ears to hear, and my heart to obey.
Strengthen my body, steady my mind, and order my steps.
I receive Your power to live, build, and overcome – today. Amen."

**Declarations for Daily Operation**

**Speak these over your life. (Say the last line three times.)**

- I operate in the Resurrection Power and Authority of Christ.
- By faith, I am in position.
- I walk in supernatural favor.
- Fresh fire of the Holy Spirit rests on me.
- Heaven fights for me; my prayers pull Heaven to earth.
- My standards rise to **excellence**.
- My faith is taking a quantum leap.
- My ground is tilled and ready for acceleration.
- God is giving me revelation for the end-time harvest.

- I see what God wants me to see.
- My mindset is aligned to the purposes of God.
- **All things are working together for my good**.
- The **Resurrection** Power of Jesus Christ is working in me now.
- The Resurrection **Power of** Jesus Christ is working in me now.
- The Resurrection Power of **Jesus Christ** is working in me now.

**Anchor Verse:**
**(Romans 8:11) – But** if the Spirit of him that raised up Jesus from the dead dwell in you, He that raised up Christ from the dead shall also quicken your mortal bodies by His Spirit that dwelleth in you.

**The Charge**

Jesus intercedes for you at the right hand of the Father; the Holy Spirit lives in you as your power source. How can you lose?
Stand up in who you are. Take the field like David. Operate at the Kingdom's Highest Levels of Value – from victory, for God's glory.

---

**God's Design for Kingdom Level Living**

**(Genesis 1:26-28)**
*"Let us make man in our image, after our likeness… and let them have dominion…"*

- We were made in God's image and likeness to **steward**, **create**, and **rule**– not to merely survive.
- Stewardship is not only about tithing (**the 10%**) but **mastering the 90%** we retain.
- To operate as Kingdom-minded stewards with dominion, we must understand **God's identity** to rightly understand **our own identity**.

**The Kingdom Levels of Value: Where You Operate Determines What You Receive**

**(Genesis 1:1-31; 2:5-7)**

God embedded value in everything He created. And within (Genesis 1 & 2), **we discover powerful spiritual patterns for wealth and purpose.**

**A. Genesis Creation Pattern (Spiritual Operating System):**

- **Create** (1:1) – God **created** heaven and earth (The 1st thing God said about Himself).
- **Move** (1:2) – Progress begins with **movement** (The Spirit Moved).
- **Speak** (1:3) – **Words** carry creative power (God spoke – we must speak).
- **See** (1:4) – **Vision** comes before manifestation (He saw – You must see what others can't see).
- **Assess & Separate** (1:4) – Discernment and holiness (**Light vs darkness**).
- **Define, Establish, and Set in Order** (1:5-6) – Structure follows revelation (**Decent and in order**).
- **Assign, Abundance, Blessings** (1:20-22) - Delegation and fruitfulness (**Multiplication**).
- **Have Dominion** (1:26) – Dominion flows from alignment with divine order (**Get in the flow**).
- **Form and Breathe Life** (2:7) – God forms us with divine purpose (**Go make an impact**).

### *Level Up Your Value*

Wealth creation is not random – it **follows predictable principles** rooted in God's Word. **The Book of Genesis lays out a divine blueprint for operating in the marketplace, building wealth, and maximizing your value. Remember this:**

- Jesus reminds us: *"**Where your treasure is**, there will your heart be also."* (Matthew 6:21)

**The truth is simple:**

- Lower Kingdom Levels of Value generate lower income.
- Higher Kingdom levels of Value generate higher income.

**The question you must ask yourself is: *At what Kingdom Level am I operating on?***

**Your Income is Tied to Your Kingdom Level of Value**

- The amount of money you make is directly connected to the Kingdom Level of Value you operate on in the marketplace.

**The Nature of Money**

- **Definition**: Money is a medium of exchange – a representation of value that flows through space and time.
- Money can exist in multiple places at once: in your account, on a card, as a check, money order, or in a digital app.
- The value of money comes from the *message it carries* and the *faith people have in it*.

**Key Kingdom Insight**: Language and faith are spiritual. And only spiritual things can be in more than one place at the same time.

---

**Spiritual Connection to Wealth**

- Money's value is a product of **belief** and **faith**.
- To increase your wealth, you must operate at a **higher spiritual level**.
- This means cultivating your ability to think, imagine, create, see and speak with intention and influence.

---

**The Framework**

Understanding these **Four Kingdoms Levels of Value (**will show us **why we earn what we earn** and **how to shift up to the next level).**

**Kingdom Level 1 – Labor (Hands) Lowest Kingdom Level of** Value

- **This is the level of labor. It's where you trade hours for dollars – working with your hands or applying a specific technical skill.**
- Scripture Insight: Paul worked as a tentmaker (Acts 18:3). Honest labor is valuable, but it should not be your final destination.
- This is where you perform the physical work yourself.
- (Genesis 2:5) – "*There was not a man to till the ground.*"
- It's much harder to get rich/wealthy at the **Lowest Kingdom Level of value**.
- The resources used at this level are **time and energy**.
- **Real Estate Example:** Operating the table saw to rehab a house, mowing lawns at your rental, or handling every tenant call yourself.
- **Example:** Truck drivers, housekeepers, food service workers, manual laborers (critical and essential workers, doing the hardest work) and they earn the least because they are **laborers - doing the work**.
- **Kingdom Principle:** Labor is good – but staying here limits multiplication. You only have so many hours in a day.

## Kingdom Level 2 – Management (Head)

At this level, you've shifted from simply using your **Hands (Labor)** to engaging your **Head** (leadership, stewardship, and decision-making). The **Head** represents wisdom, order, and strategy – the ability to coordinate, align, and multiply resources through management.

### What the Head Represents

- **Strategic Thinking** – Instead of doing everything, you begin to design systems. You're thinking about *how* things should get done, not just doing them.
- **Delegation** – You place the right people in the right roles. A good head doesn't try to be the hands, feet, or mouth – it directs each part to function properly.
- **Stewardship** – You manage money, time, and talent wisely, multiplying resources instead of exhausting them.
- **Vision Alignment** – The head sees where the body is going. **Management** at this level is about keeping people aligned with the mission.
- Kingdom Principle at the ***Head:*** - *"Moreover it is required in stewards, that a man be found faithful."* (1 Corinthians 4:2)
- The **Head** is not about control – it's about stewardship. When you prove faithful in managing resources and people at Level 2, God can entrust you with greater influence at Level 3 and greater **Vision** at Level 4.

- **Scripture Insight:** Joseph was elevated to manage Pharaoh's resources and lead an entire nation through famine (Genesis 41:39–41).

- **Kingdom Principle:** Stewardship multiplies results. Instead of one person working, you now orchestrate many.

- Managers earn more than the people they oversee, but still less than those operating at Kingdom Levels 3 & 4.

- **Example**: A manager of a tire shop might earn $40K–$90K/year, while a manager at Microsoft might earn $300K/year.
- **Real Estate Example:** Hiring a property manager, working with contractors, building a team.

**Summary:**
The **Management (Head)** in **Level 2** is the seat of wisdom, stewardship, and strategy. It's where you stop thinking like a worker and start thinking like a manager. It multiplies effort through people, systems, and alignment. And it's the proving ground for Levels 3 and 4 – because until you can steward people and resources, you won't be trusted with greater influence and vision.

**Kingdom Level 3 – Influence (Voice)**

- **This is a critical turning point in the *Kingdom Levels of Value* framework, because it's the level where multiplication accelerates beyond what the Hands (Level 1) and Head (Level 2) can ever produce.**
- At **Kingdom Level 3**, your **Voice** becomes the most valuable asset you possess. **Influence** is about **moving people, shaping environments, and unlocking opportunities with your words, leadership, and presence.**
- This is where you shift from managing systems and people to **inspiring them**, casting vision, and mobilizing resources. At this level, your value is no longer measured by how much work you do – but by how many lives you can impact and move into action.
- **Life and Death in Words** – *"Death and life are in the power of the tongue"* (Proverbs 18:21). **Your words carry Kingdom weight to build or destroy**.

**What the Voice Represents**

- **Persuasion and Communication** – Influence is birthed when you can clearly articulate vision and value.
- **Authority and Leadership** – A strong voice carries authority that people recognize and follow.

- **Teaching and Storytelling** – Voice transmits wisdom, experience, and faith to others in a way that multiplies impact.
- **Networking and Relationships** – The right words spoken at the right time open doors money can't buy.

**Real Estate Examples of the Voice**

- **Raising Capital** – Instead of using only your own money, you present opportunities and attract investors.
- **Negotiation** – Deals are won or lost at the table, not on the construction site. Your words create terms that build wealth.
- **Teaching & Coaching** – Hosting a workshop, podcast, or seminar where your teaching inspires others – and positions you as a thought leader.
- **Leadership** – Rallying contractors, managers, and partners around a shared vision of excellence.
- At this level, you stop working *in* real estate and start working *through* influence.

**Kingdom Principle of Influence**

- ***"Now therefore go, and I will be with thy mouth, and teach thee what thou shalt say."*** (Exodus 4:12)
- Moses didn't lead Israel out of Egypt with his hands – but with his **voice**, backed by God's authority. Kingdom influence isn't manipulation – it's Spirit-led communication that aligns people with God's purpose.

**Why Level 3 is Critical**

- **Scalability** – **Labor** (Level 1) and **Management** (Level 2) are limited by time and team size. **Voice** (Level 3) can reach thousands – or millions – at once.
- **Leverage** – **Influence** allows you to attract resources, opportunities, and partnerships far beyond your personal capacity.

- **Preparation for Vision** – Before God entrusts you with Level 4 **(Vision)**, He tests your ability to use your voice faithfully at Level 3.

**Call to Action for Readers**

- **Ask yourself:**
- Am I hiding my **Voice**, or am I developing it as a tool of **Influence**?
- **Do I use my words** to tear down, or to build faith, unity, and wealth?
- **Am I intentionally learning communication skills** (public speaking, teaching, negotiation), or am I letting opportunities pass me by?

- **Scripture Insight:** Jesus spoke with authority, and multitudes followed Him (Mark 1:22, Matthew 7:28–29). His words created alignment, faith, and action.

- God speaks **(Voice)** with influence: *"God said, Let there be light."* (Genesis 1:3)

- Kingdom Principle: (Proverbs 18:21) says, "Death and life are in the power of the tongue." When you step into **Influence**, your voice shapes markets, relationships, and legacies.

**How to Get There:**

- Develop your vocal skills and your ability to influence. Learn to articulate value, not just deliver it.

- Build credibility through integrity and results. Influence flows through trust.

- **Recognize that your story, testimony, and vision are currency. The way you tell them opens doors.**

**Key Insight**: **Real wealth begins at this level** – authors, speakers, and influencers often earn millions because they move the masses.

**Kingdom Level 4 – Vision (Spirit) The Highest Kingdom Level of Value**

- **This is where everything in your framework comes together – where revelation and imagination meet stewardship and influence, and where wealth shifts from *what you do* to *what you see.***
- At **Level 4**, you step into the realm of **Spirit-led vision, divine creativity, and generational impact.** This is the place of **revelation**, where God allows you to *see what others cannot see* and create what others could not imagine.
- While **Level 3 (Voice)** multiplies influence, **Level 4 multiplies creation.** Visionaries birth new possibilities into existence. They don't just work the system – they design the future.
- **This is the Highest Kingdom Level** – where you shift from income to *impact*. Vision is imagination fueled by revelation. It's where God downloads ideas and strategies that others can't see.
- **Scripture Insight: "Write the vision, and make it plain**…" (Habakkuk 2:2). Abraham was told to look up at the stars and see his inheritance before it existed (Genesis 15:5). **Vision precedes manifestation**.
- **Real Estate Example:** Instead of flipping one house, you design a build-to-rent community. In addition to buying properties, you create trusts and strategies that position your children's children for generational wealth (Proverbs 13:22). Instead of just joining the market, you change it.
- **Kingdom Principle:** Vision is where Heaven touches earth. It is the birthplace of transformation. This is where you stop thinking about what you can afford and start thinking about what you can ***create***.

**Biblical Foundation of Vision (Spirit)**

- **(Habakkuk 2:2)** – *"Write the vision, and make it plain upon tables, that he may run that readeth it."* Vision is not just for seeing – it is for directing others into purpose.
- **(Genesis 15:5)** – God told Abram to *look up at the stars* to see his inheritance before it became reality. Faith required a visionary lens.
- **(Proverbs 29:18)** – *"Where there is no vision, the people perish."* Vision preserves life, purpose, and destiny.
- **(Nehemiah 4:5)** – Before a wall was rebuilt, a vision was cast. His leadership flowed from Spirit-driven sight.

**What the Spirit (Vision) Represents**

- **Revelation** – Seeing with spiritual eyes what others miss with natural eyes.
  **Creativity** – Innovation inspired by Heaven – new strategies, models, and ideas.
- **Legacy Thinking** – Vision stretches beyond today's needs to shape the destiny of future generations.
- **Alignment with God's Purpose** – Vision is not mere ambition - it's Heaven's blueprint revealed on earth.

---

**Real Estate Examples of Vision (Spirit)**

- **From Deals to Developments** – Instead of buying one house, you design entire communities that serve Kingdom purposes (e.g., affordable housing with dignity).
- Build-to-Rent Models – While others see houses, you see generational income streams.
- **Kingdom Legacy Structures** – Trusts, endowments, or nonprofit entities that ensure your wealth outlives you.

- **Redemptive Vision –** Taking blighted properties and seeing what they *can become* – not just financially, but for Kingdom transformation of communities.

---

**Kingdom Principle of Vision**

- *"Call unto me, and I will answer thee, and shew thee great and mighty things, which thou knowest not."* (Jeremiah 33:3)
- Vision is a download from Heaven. It's not just creativity or brainstorming – it's alignment with divine insight. God gives vision to those who are faithful stewards at the lower levels because He knows they will carry it out with integrity.

---

**Why Level 4 is the Highest Level**

- **Unlimited Multiplication** – Your hands can only build so much, and your head can only manage so many people. Your voice can reach across nations, and your *vision can* create entire new realities. Vision multiplies beyond time, place, and person – leaving legacies that can outlive you for generations.
- **Market Shaping** – You don't just react to economic shifts – you redefine them. You don't wait for trends – you set them. True wealth builders anticipate, innovate, and create the very lanes others will later follow.
- **Kingdom Advancement** – Vision-driven believers bring Heaven's culture to earth – through business, real estate, ministry, and legacy.

---

**How to Access Vision (Spirit)**

- Prayer and Intimacy with God – **Revelation comes from His presence, not pressure**.
- Fasting and Focus – **Create space for God's Spirit to reveal fresh direction**.

- Journaling and Writing – **Capture vision clearly so others can run with it**.
- Surround Yourself with Visionaries – Iron sharpens iron; **you rise to the level of those who see higher than you see**.
- Obedience in Small Things – Stewardship at Kingdom Levels 1–3 will position you for **greater Vision at Kingdom Level 4**.

---

**Call to Action for Readers**

**Ask yourself:**

- Am I living only by what I see naturally, or am I cultivating spiritual sight?
- Am I building just for income, or am I shaping a legacy that will outlive me?
- Am I writing down and communicating the visions God has given me, or am I letting them fade away?

**Summary:**
**Vision (Spirit)** is the **Highest Kingdom Level of Value** because it births the unseen into reality. It is where revelation meets innovation, and where wealth shifts from being temporary to eternal. At this level, you are no longer defined by the market, your labor, or even your voice – you **are defined by what Heaven reveals to you and what you dare to build in alignment with that vision**.

*** What are you creating with the mind of Christ in YOU?**

**The Shift: From Effort to Multiplication**

- At Level 1 **(Labor)** You earn what your *hands* can produce.
- At Level 2 **(Management)** You earn what a *team* can produce under your stewardship.

- At Level 3 **(Influence)** You earn **what your *voice* and *leadership* can produce.**
- At Level 4 (Vision) – You earn **what your *ideas and revelation* can produce.**

**The progression is clear: as you move up, your income and impact grow, not because you're working harder, but because you're working at a Higher Kingdom Level of Value.**

---

### The Impact of Kingdom Levels 3 and 4

This is where the ***"Wealth Code"*** is truly **Unlocked**. Kingdom Levels 1 and 2 will pay your bills, but Levels 3 and 4 will build your *legacy*.

The "Wealth Code" is not about hustling harder – it's about ascending into Levels 3 and 4, where faith, gifts, and vision converge to produce exponential impact.

---

### Identity in Christ & Purpose

- What are you believing God for in this journey?
- It begins with knowing your **identity in Christ**.
- **(1 Chronicles 29:11)** – God's power and majesty overall.
- **(Jeremiah 1:5)** – God set you apart and appointed you.

---

### Dominion Mandate

- **(Genesis 1:26)** – Created to have dominion over the earth.
- Purpose: To extend God's rule and authority on earth.
- **(John 10:10)** – Jesus came to give abundant life.
- **(Romans 8:37)** – We are more than conquerors.

---

**Overcoming Limitations**

- Excuses: not smart enough, lack of education, etc.
- **(Luke 10:19)** – Authority over all power of the enemy.
- **(1 John 4:4)** – Greater is He in you.
- **(Isaiah 55:8–13)** – God's thoughts are higher than ours.

---

**Our True Identity**

- Made in the image and likeness of Christ (Ephesians 2:10).
- I can do all things through Christ (Philippians 4:13).
- Equipped with the Holy Spirit (Romans 8:9).
- Called to reflect God's awesomeness (1 John 4:17).
- More than conquerors through Christ (Romans 8:37).
- The Resurrected King of Glory lives inside of us (1 John 4:4).
- He has made us the Head and not the tail (Deuteronomy 28:13).
- Greater is Christ in us than he that is in the world (1 John 4:4).

---

If you're in Level 3, your platform can fuel generational wealth. If you're at Level 4, your assets **already are**.

Many successful people bounce between the two. The key is to **stay intentional** about growing your ownership while expanding your influence.

**Final Thought: Don't Settle – Go Higher**

The path to Kingdom Level 3 and Kingdom Level 4 isn't always easy. It takes courage, risk, vision, and patience. But the rewards are **exponential**.

**Start asking yourself:**

- What am I building that will outlive me?
- What can I own, not just operate?
- How can I use my influence to create wealth?

**And never forget:**

**The Higher Kingdom Level you go, the more your ideas – not your hours – create wealth.**

This is how you shift from laborer to leader… from manager to mogul… from someone who makes money to someone who **multiplies money**.

And the journey continues.

---

**Next: Let's talk about managing what you've built – and why the 90% matters more than most people realize.**

# Chapter 4

## Managing the 90% - The Stewardship Advantage

*(With Case Studies & Real-Life Testimony)*

---

**Theme Scriptures:** [10] *He that is faithful in that which is least is faithful also in much: and he that is unjust in the least is unjust also in much.* [11] *If therefore ye have not been faithful in the unrighteous mammon, who will commit to your trust the true riches?* [12] *And if ye have not been faithful in that which is another man's, who shall give you that which is your own?* ***(Luke 16:10-12)***

### The Hidden Side of Kingdom Wealth

For many believers, the tithe is familiar territory – the sacred first 10% we return to God as an act of obedience, worship, and faith. It is the covenant handshake between Heaven and Earth. It activates protection, rebukes the devourer, and positions us for blessings.

**But here's the uncomfortable truth:**
***The tithe alone will not make you wealthy.*** **"Why is that Coach?"**

**Tithing is covenant alignment – it honors God as the Source** and opens the windows of heaven (Malachi 3:10) – but **the tithe alone won't build wealth.** Wealth grows when giving and stewardship work together. Jesus' parable of the talents shows that resources were distributed **"according to their ability,"** and increase came to the servants who managed, multiplied, and reported faithfully (Matthew 25:14–30; Luke 16:10). In other words, God doesn't just hand out money; **He gives the power to get wealth** - ideas, discipline, skill, and favor to those who develop capacity (Deuteronomy 8:18). **That's why the 90% matters so much: learn the tools and skillsets – budgeting, cash flow, reserves, underwriting deals, negotiation, team-building, and asset selection** so your dollars are assigned, not wandering; invested, and not wasted. As you give, **God "ministers seed to the sower"**

and multiplies what you steward (2 Corinthians 9:10), **but it's your ability and management that determine how far that blessing flows**.

**Think of it like planting seeds in good soil** – that's the tithe. But without water, sunlight, and consistent care – that's stewardship – those seeds will never produce their full harvest.

The **tithe opens the windows** of Heaven – a truth proclaimed in pulpits and synagogues across the world. **Yet,** in my experience, **far too little is taught about what happens next: how to manage, increase, and multiply the remaining 90%.** ***This gap must close***. For while the tithe unlocks Heaven's supply, **it is stewardship that determines how much of that blessing flows into your life – to build wealth and advance the Kingdom**. **"Give, and it shall be** given unto you; good measure, pressed down, shaken together, and **running over…"** (Luke 6:38)

**The Joseph Principle: Management Before Promotion**

When famine hit Egypt, millions starved across the region – but Egypt thrived. Why? Because Joseph didn't just hear from God, he **managed** what God gave him.

God gave Pharaoh a dream. Joseph gave Pharaoh a plan.
The dream was revelation - the plan was stewardship.

- In years of plenty, Joseph stored up grain.
- In years of famine, Egypt had more than enough.
- Joseph didn't just bless Egypt; he became a channel of blessing to nations.

**Here's the key:** God promoted Joseph not because he was the most gifted dreamer, but because he could **manage resources wisely under pressure.**

**If God gave you double your income today, would your life double in impact – or double in debt (more stuff)?**

***"Tithing opens the window. Stewardship determines what flows through it."***

### The Kingdom Compound Effect

Start Small. Stay Consistent. Let Time Do the Heavy Lifting.

**Let's keep it real:** if you understand compound interest, you're positioned to collect it. If you don't, you'll spend life paying it.

Compound interest means you earn interest on your money, and on the interest your money already earned. Picture a small snowball at the top of a hill. Every roll adds more snow, which makes it bigger, which helps it collect even more with the next roll. That's compounding.

### Two simple truths you can bank on

- Start early. Time is the multiplier you can't buy later.
- Stay steady. Small, regular deposits often beat occasional big ones.

### The Everyday Investor's Game Plan

#### 1) Automate it (so you don't "forget")

Set a recurring transfer the day after payday. Even $50–$200 per paycheck builds momentum. Treat it like a bill you pay to your future self.

#### 2) Dollar-Cost Averaging (DCA)

**Invest the same dollar amount on a schedule (weekly or monthly) no matter what prices are doing.**

- When prices dip, your money buys more shares.
- When prices rise, your money buys fewer shares.
- Over time, your average cost smooths out, and you stay in the game.

**3) Where to put it (simple beats fancy)**

- Index Funds/ETFs (e.g., broad market funds) for hands-off growth.
- Target-date funds inside a 401(k)/403(b)/IRA if you want a one-fund solution.
- Growth vs. Value Funds: growth aims for faster expansion; value hunts for strong companies priced below their worth. Many investors own both through a broad index fund.

**4) Buy & Hold (the long game)**

Markets move up and down daily but generally march up over decades. Decide your time horizon now: 10+ years. That decision will save you from panic-selling later. **Remember: Buy Low, Sell High**.

**Quick story:** My granddaughter wanted $180 Nike shoes **(I let her know that only people with a job or income buy those)**. I also let her know that I like Nikes too – but I like them more as a shareholder. I always buy Nikes when they are on sale. I showed her the stock price and explained dividends. "Own enough shares, and the dividends can buy your shoes. Now your assets pay for your liabilities." That's a new mindset (owner mindset).

When dealing with the Stock Market **(Buy Low - Sell High).**

---

**Real Estate: Leverage, But Do It Wisely**

**Leverage is using other people's money (the bank's) to control a larger asset. It magnifies results – good and bad.**

A clear, no-hype example

You have $100,000 to invest.

**Option A – One house, all cash:**

- Buy 1 property at $100,000.
- If values rise 20% in a year: $100,000 → $120,000 (gain $20,000).
- Year 2: another 20% on $120,000 → $144,000 (gain $24,000).

**Option B – Five houses with 20% down each (leverage):**

- Control $500,000 of property with your $100,000 down; bank finances $400,000.
- Year 1 at +20%: $500,000 → $600,000 (equity ↑ by $100,000).
- Year 2 at +20%: $600,000 → $720,000 (equity ↑ by another $120,000).

**Why the big difference? You owned more assets. But remember: if prices fall, leverage magnifies losses too.**

**Guardrails for wise leverage**

- Favor fixed-rate loans in rising-rate environments.
- Insist on cash flow (rents cover mortgage, taxes, insurance, maintenance, reserves).
- Stress test each property: would it still break even if rent dropped 10–15% or vacancy rose, or (30% over your entire portfolio)?
- Keep 3–6 months of expenses per property in cash reserves.

---

**Kingdom Moves (Mindset + Mechanics)**

**1) Tithes and stewardship of the 90%.**
Honor God first, then manage the rest with purpose: create, invest, trade, produce, multiply.

**2) The 10-Year Focus.**
Ten years of consistent sowing (learning + doing) can change your whole financial lineage. **Most "overnight successes" spent a decade staying faithful.**

**3) Health is wealth.**
You are the engine of your assignments. Move your body 3 – 4 times a week. Eat like your calling matters. High energy = high capacity to build.

**4) Influence (Voice) & Vision (Operate at the Kingdom highest levels).**

- Influence sells your ideas, negotiates deals, and raises capital. Practice it– join a speaking club, teach, or present regularly.
- Vision designs offers, systems, and solutions. Ask daily: *"Lord, show me what You want me to see– even what others can't see."*
  Then sketch the vision, strategize, and take the first step.

---

**Faith-Fueled Multiplication: The Laws of Sowing & Reaping**

1. You must sow before you reap. Start where you are – today.
2. You reap what you sow. Plant education, discipline, and assets; reap wisdom, capacity, and cash flow.
3. You reap more than you sow. Multiplication takes time – water the seed with consistent action.

"**Remember this:** Whoever sows sparingly will also reap sparingly, and whoever sows generously will also reap generously." (2 Corinthians 9:6)

---

**Quick Wins for This Week**

- Turn on auto-investing (even $50/week).
- Open (or increase) your 401(k)/IRA contribution enough to capture the employer match – that's **free money**.
- List every expense for 30 days. Find one recurring "leak" and redirect it to your investment.
- Read 30 minutes/day on finance, investing or real estate. (The seed is knowledge. The harvest is options.)
- Walk or drive one neighborhood you'd invest in. Run the numbers on two listings.
- Book a credit check-up; create a plan to lift your score (secured card, on-time payments, lower utilization).

**A Word on Interest Rates (Don't be scared) Run the numbers**

Rates move in cycles. Some of us bought our first homes at double-digit interest **(12.5% for my 1st home)**. Yes, lower is better – but you can still build in higher-rate seasons:

- Buy right (price + cash flow).
- Fix the rate when possible.
- Refinance later if/when rates fall.
- Improve the asset to force equity (repairs, energy upgrades, better management).

**Declarations (Say it out loud)**

- **I sow consistently; I reap abundantly.**
- **I start small and I start now.**
- **My money works while I sleep.**
- **I use leverage wisely and keep strong reserves.**
- **I communicate with clarity and I imagine with faith.**
- **I'm playing the long game - and time is on my side.**

**Interviewer: Dr. Leon, why put *money* and *ministry* in the same conversation? A lot of churches separate the two.**

**Dr. Leon:** There aren't two kingdoms - *church life* and *business life*. There's one Kingdom. God cares how we earn, steward, and multiply just as much as how we worship. **If we only preach "give," but never teach "budget, build, invest, multiply and steward the 90%," we set people up to struggle. Kingdom stewardship is worship in motion**.

**Power Points:**

- One Kingdom, not two.
- Give first. Steward the 90%. Invest. Multiply to bless.

---

**Interviewer: You often say, "Lord, help me see what others can't." Where did that come from?**

**Dr. Leon: From hunger. I started praying:**

"**Lord, help me see what You want me to see** – even what others can't see. Help me hear what You're saying – even what others don't."

**Then God proved it**. My wife and I were walking in Alexandria, VA. We passed a property that looked like a junkyard – old buses, cars, needle caps, and dog houses. Terrible. But when I looked at the property, I could see a mansion on a beautiful estate lot – value hidden under clutter.

I met the owner, negotiated owner financing (small down, annual payments, 5-year balloon), cleared the lot with a front-end loader and dump truck, and boom - the neighborhood said, **"I never realized how beautiful this land is!"** *We doubled our money in just over a year.*

**Quote:** ***"Often the value is there - the clutter is just louder."***

**Path Forward (Land/Deal Vision):**

1) Walk & pray. 2) Ask about owner financing. 3) Clear the clutter (physical or paperwork). 4) Add simple value. 5) Exit wisely.

---

**Interviewer:** People love that story, but many feel stuck – paycheck to paycheck. Where do they even start?

**Dr. Leon: Start simple and honest.**

1. List every bill. All of them.
2. Build a budget you can actually live with.

3. Cut one non-essential bill (even temporarily).
4. Take the **free money** – if **your job's 401K/403b matches your retirement contributions, contribute to the match at least**.
5. Automate a small savings transfer.
6. Build toward having a minimum of 3 sources of income **(the 3-legged stool as my favorite Uncle "D" would say)**.
7. Serve someone every week. Sowing breaks the fear cycle.

**Power Point:** ***Small, consistent steps beat big, inconsistent promises.***

**Interviewer:** What about someone who lost a house or feels they've "missed it"?

**Dr. Leon:** Start again. We helped our daughter get started. She thought she needed a "perfect" credit score. No, she needed a clear plan.

**The "Get-On-Track" Plan:**

- Meet a lender now. Don't wait to be perfect. Ask, "Where am I today, and what would qualify me?"
- If needed, get a secured card (small limit). Use it for gas/groceries only; pay in full monthly to build/improve your credit.
- Stabilize income and reduce debt-to-income.
- Walk/ride neighborhoods and pray: "Lord, show me what others don't see."
- Shop below market; look for value you can add (paint, cleanup, finish a basement).
- Move when peace + pre-approval + property align.

**She did this, got pre-approved, and bought a solid brick home below market on a big lot. Vision + steps = keys in hand.**

**Interviewer: You've been called and ordained as an "Apostle to the Marketplace." What does that look like day to day?**

**Dr. Leon:** For me, it's carrying Good News into the business arena – outside the four walls of the church. Day to day, that looks like coaching and mentoring, creating jobs, investing with integrity, and being ready to pray for people wherever I am – yes, even in a grocery line if the Holy Spirit leads me. Jesus preached in the marketplace as much as in the synagogues, and I feel most alive when I follow Him into those ordinary places and watch Him do extraordinary things.

My wife and I founded Lighthouse Marketplace Ministries, and even the name is prophetic. *Lighthouse* – because we are called to be a light that points the way, helping people find safety, clarity, and direction while we build and advance the Kingdom. *Marketplace* – because the assignment is to make a Kingdom impact everywhere we go, beyond Sunday services and church walls.

Practically, that means ministering inside the church and outside of it – training, equipping, teaching, and activating everyone within my sphere of influence to impact and reclaim the marketplace for Jesus Christ. It's praying with a contractor on a job site, negotiating a deal with fairness when cutting corners would be easier, paying vendors on time because righteousness matters, and helping entrepreneurs steward their businesses so they bless families and communities.

How do I feel when I'm walking in that purpose? Settled. Joyful. Strong. I feel the weight of responsibility, but it's a "light yoke" because it fits – like it was made for me. There's a deep sense of alignment, like my spirit saying, *this is what you were built for.* When I'm coaching and doing mock interviews to help a member land a new position, get a promotion, or when a cashier asks for prayer and leaves with hope - those are the moments I know I'm exactly where God wants me. That's what being an Apostle to the Marketplace looks like in my life, day by day carrying His presence into real work, with real people, for real impact.

**Power Points:**

- **Marketplace "less religious."**
- **Your workplace and/or business is a pulpit. Your excellence is a witness.**

---

**Interviewer:** Some obstacles aren't financial, they're internal. How do you address those?

**Dr. Leon:** You're right. Invisible barriers: fear, scarcity thinking, and bitterness - block blessings. We **break them** with truth, prayer, and small brave actions.

**3 Breakers:**

1. **Truth:** "I'm- a steward and a builder, not just a consumer."
2. **Prayer:** "Lord, break every invisible barrier; open my eyes to hidden value."
3. **Action:** One courageous step daily – call the lender, cancel or reduce your cable, open the secured card, walk or drive the neighborhood.

**Interviewer:** Give us five moves people can take *this week.*

**Dr. Leon:**

1. Pray 5 minutes each morning: "Lord, show me today's opportunity."
2. Money snapshot: List bills/income; make one move (cancel one expense, add $50 to savings, pay $50 to a debt).
3. Credit builder: If needed, open a secured card; use for one category; pay in full monthly.
4. Walk & watch, drive & watch: Visit one target area; note 3 properties with obvious cleanup or paint needs.
5. Book a lender call: Turn their advice into a 90-day plan.

**Quote: *"God meets you in motion."***

---

**Interviewer:** Last word to the reader who wants to thrive, not just survive?

**Dr. Leon: Declare this with me -**

- *I live in one Kingdom - Sunday through Saturday.*
- *I steward the 90% with wisdom; I multiply to bless.*
- *God opens my eyes to hidden value.*
- ***Fear and poverty mindsets are broken off my life.***
- *I won't just survive; I will thrive – and help others do the same.*

**Prayer:**
"Father, thank You for wisdom and courage. Break every invisible barrier. Teach my hands to build, my heart to steward, and my eyes to see value where others see junk. Order my steps. Use me in the marketplace for Your glory. In Jesus' name, amen."

---

**Bonus: Interview Lightning Round**

Q: First wealth habit to start today?
A: Automate $25–$100 to savings; you'll adjust and never miss it.

Q: One sentence that changes deals?
A: "What's the least you'd take if we could close quickly?"

Q: How do I know it's the right move?
A: Peace + numbers work + wise counsel aligns.

Q: What if I'm scared?
A: Move *small* – but move. Courage grows with reps.

---

**Your path forward is clear: Ask. Act. Adjust. Repeat.**
Clear the clutter – watch the value appear.

### Why the 90% Holds the Key

When you tithe, the blessing is released. But **the *management* of the remaining 90% determines whether that blessing multiplies, stagnates, or even disappears**.

(Malachi 3:10) makes a promise that God will open the windows of Heaven and pour out blessings we cannot contain. But think about this: what happens if God pours out blessings and we have no system, no discipline, no structure to handle them?

Blessing without management leads to waste.
Management without blessing leads to struggle.
But blessing **and** management lead to multiplication.

---

### From Widow's Oil to Overflow

**In 2 Kings 4, a widow was drowning in debt.** Her creditors were coming to take her sons as slaves. In desperation, she cried out to the prophet Elisha for help.

**Now notice this: *Elisha didn't give her money*. Neither did he take up an offering**. Instead, **he gave her something much greater – a management strategy.**

1. **Take Inventory – "*What do you have in your house?*"** She thought she had nothing but a little oil. But Elisha forced her to see that what she did have was enough to start. God always begins with what's already in your hand. That's why **the first skill you need is awareness: inventorying your resources, your abilities, your relationships, your assets. Sometimes the seed for your breakthrough is already sitting in your house.**

2. **Leverage Relationships – "*Go borrow vessels from your neighbors.*"** Here's wisdom: when you don't have capacity, borrow it. The widow had oil, but no containers. You may have the skill but not the platform, the idea but not the financing, the drive but not the team.

Leverage relationships and partnerships to expand your capacity. **Networking, credibility, and trust are Kingdom tools just as important as money.**

3. **Work the Plan – "*Pour the oil.*" This was the active part.** No excuses, no delays – she had to take action. That's a management skill: execution. **Plans and ideas are useless until they're poured out. Think about it: the oil didn't multiply in storage - it multiplied in the pouring.** Your gifts, talents, and business ideas multiply as you *use* them, not as you sit on them. **Note: Be careful who you share your plan with (on a need-to-know-basis-only).**

4. **Manage the Profit – "*Sell the oil, pay your debts, and live on the rest.*"** Elisha gave her a financial plan: eliminate debt, generate income, and create sustainability. **This wasn't just about a one-time bailout - it was about positioning her for overflow.** She went from drowning in debt to having a business that could sustain her family **(generational wealth).**

**This wasn't just a miracle – it was a masterclass in stewardship.** God's multiplication met her management. **The oil was the miracle, but the vessels, the pouring, and the selling were the management skills.**

**The same principle applies to us today.** God may not hand you a bag of cash, **but He's already placed something in your hand – a** property, a skill, a network, an idea. **The question is: *Will you inventory it, leverage it, pour it, and manage it well enough for Him to multiply it?***

**The Borrowed Boat – Obedience wins the day (God Uses What's Already in Your Hands) (*Luke 5:1–11*)**

Jesus borrows Simon's boat to teach the crowd, then tells this tired pro (professional fisherman) to "launch out into the deep and let down your nets." Though they'd caught nothing all night, Simon had **a nevertheless moment** - choosing obedience over expertise – **"at thy word"** he let down the net and it exploded with fish, so full two boats nearly sink. Jesus blessed him beyond what he could have ever image. He was so impacted by this overwhelming supernatural provision for his family and partner that he fell to his knees. Jesus promoted him on the spot to be one of His disciples.

**Teaching lessons (put these to work):**

- Obedience > expertise: do it God's way even when it defies experience.
- Go deeper: breakthroughs live beyond comfortable, shallow water.

**Kingdom Math: Blessed 90% > Cursed 100%**

Here's a divine paradox: 90% blessed will always go further than 100% without God's covering.

That's why people can make six or seven figures and still be broke – because without God's blessing and their own stewardship, their 100% is eaten up by debt, poor spending habits, and missed opportunities.

**But a person who tithes and manages the 90% well will see doors open, opportunities arise, and their resources stretch in supernatural ways.**

**My Mentee Turned $500 into a $90,000 Asset**

I once coached a gentleman who made decent money but lived paycheck to paycheck. We began managing the 90%, and we put a **four-part plan** in place:

1. Eliminate bad debt.
2. Create a "seed fund" for investments.
3. Improve credit score to 700 or above.
4. Focus on income-producing assets.

Within 18 months, he turned $500 saved each month into a $90,000 rental property – and that property has produced rental income (with cash-flow) every single month since.

He didn't just get a pay raise; he got a wealth building strategy.

**The Stewardship Mindset**

Stewardship is not ownership.
Everything you have belongs to God. Your role is to manage it faithfully, multiply it wisely, and use it for Kingdom purposes.

**Five core principles:**

1. Tithing Redeems the Rest – The first portion makes the rest holy.
2. Stewardship > Ownership – We are managers of God's resources.
3. Blessed Portion > Full Portion – 90% blessed will outperform 100% without God.
4. First Things First – God must be first in both giving and managing.
5. **Tithing is Worship** – It's a heart decision, not a financial transaction. **Can God trust you with His…?**

---

**How to Make Money Work for You**

**This is where the shift happens.** You stop working **for** money and start putting your money to **work for you**.

**Here are examples:**

- Buying cash-flowing real estate.
- Starting an online business that runs while you sleep.
- Investing in dividend-producing stocks.
- Creating products or intellectual property (IP) that pay royalties.
- Automating your savings and investments so wealth builds on autopilot.

---

### The Shift That Changes Everything

This isn't just about money. It's about **destiny**.

When you manage the 90% well:

- You sleep better.
- You give more.
- You dream bigger.
- You walk in greater peace.
- You impact more lives.

You don't just **earn** more – you **become** more.

God is raising up a remnant who won't just survive – they'll **steward**, **multiply**, and **advance the Kingdom**.

He's using people like you – and voices like mine – to **reveal what hasn't been taught**, to activate what's been dormant, and to shift people from paycheck-to-paycheck… to overflow-to-overflow.

---

### Stewardship Unlocks Increase

Here's how Kingdom multiplication works:

1. **You tithe (or give generously)** – opening the windows of Heaven.
2. **You manage the 90% with wisdom** – showing God you're trustworthy.
3. **You increase your ability** – reading, learning, building systems.
4. **You get more** – not by accident, but by alignment.
5. **You multiply** – leveraging people, capital, and opportunities.
6. **You give again** – and the cycle grows bigger each time.

**Manage the 90% - Having a *practical, faith-driven talk with YOU***

"Tithing opens the window. **Stewardship of the 90%** determines what flows through it."

---

**In my introduction, I told you this book was more about you than me: Let's talk for a minute.**

**Why This Talk Matters**

**If you've ever said, "I tithe... but I'm still stressed about money," or "I'm still living paycheck to paycheck", this is for you.**
Most churches teach the **10%** (and amen to that), but almost no one teaches how to **manage the 90%**. Let's **fix that** – today.

**Goal of this talk:** show you how to turn your 90% into **assets, cash flow, and legacy -** without hype and with God's wisdom.

---

**The Big Truth (Bible & Basics)**

- **(Matthew 25:15)** – God **entrusts** wealth "according to our **ability**." **So... increase your ability**.
- **(Proverbs 10:22)** – The blessing of the Lord **makes rich** and adds no sorrow.
- Tithing is obedience. **Stewardship** is responsibility. Both matters.

**Plain talk:**

- **Assets** put money **in** your pocket (cash flow, equity, dividends).
- **Liabilities** take money **out** (payments, subscriptions, lifestyle creep).
- **Income follows assets.**
- **Being broke follows liabilities.**

---

## Where Your 90% Is Going (and What To Do Next)

Ask yourself: *"Where is the money God gave me?"*
Is it going to rent (building someone else's asset)?
To a nicer car, more eating out, endless streaming, hair/nails, tennis shoes, boots, the newest phone?

There's nothing wrong with nice things. But let **assets pay for the toys** – not the other way around.

**Simple Reframe:**

1. **Build/pay for assets first.**
2. Let **assets pay** for lifestyle later.

---

## The 30-Day Money Map

**Do this for one month** (it will change everything):

1. **Write down every expense** (no guilt, just honesty).
2. Circle what **builds** you (shelter, skill, savings) vs. what **drains** you.
3. Keep the essentials; **trim one financial leak** a week.
4. Set a **small automatic transfer** to savings (even $25-$50).

You can't lead what you won't first **measure**.

---

## Redeem the "5–10 PM Window"

Most of us work 9–5 building **someone else's** dream. Use **5–10 PM** to build **yours**:

- Learn a money-making-money **skillset** (YouTube/Google Univ, AI).
- Launch a **simple service** (car/detail, window wash, delivery, tutoring, cleaning, etc.).
- Create an **offer** people actually need right now.

- Repeat the prayer: *"Lord, show me what others don't see."*

---

**If You Hate Budgets… Do This**

Budget + Raise Income = Best of both worlds. But if budgets make you itch:

- Keep the **Money Map** (tracking, not pinching).
- Add **one new income stream** (Uber, Instacart, small services, digital help).
- **Automate** 5–10% of every dollar to savings/investing.

---

**Free Money You Might Be Ignoring**

- If your job matches **401(k)/403(b)** contributions (5–6% is common), that's **free money**.
- Start at the match. Automate it. Adjust your life around it. Years from now you'll thank yourself and me – like my friend **Bishop "T" who built a multiple six-figure 401K retirement account just by starting and being consistent (I gave him the play - he ran the play)**.

**Your First Real Estate Move (Clear & Doable)**

You don't need to start with an apartment building. Start with a **home**.

**Five Steps to First Keys:**

1. **Meet a lender now** (don't wait to be "perfect"). Ask: "Where am I today? What would qualify me?"
2. **Build/repair credit** (secured card for gas/groceries, pay in full).
3. **Save** a modest cushion (closing costs + a month or two).
4. **Walk or drive neighborhoods (inner city or rural & pray).** Look for value you can **add** (paint, clean-up, finish a basement).

5. Consider **house hacking** (rent a room or two so the house pays for itself – sacrifice now/drop your pride and do what you got to do, to get to where you want to be). My daughter and granddaughter did this. Today they own homes with **six-figure equity in the house**, and payment **less than local rents**. When will you get started? **STOP whining about not wanting to live with anybody else - when you're broke**. *Do it for a season and reap the harvest.*

**Position Beats Luck**

Opportunities find people who are **ready**:

- **Cash cushion** (even small).
- **Credit steps** in motion.
- **Skill** growing (YouTube/Google Univ, AI).
- **Eyes open** (you're out walking, driving, calling, asking).

God meets you **in motion**, not just in meditation.

**Faith That Works (Not Just Talks)**

- **Work the Word.**
- **Actionable faith** = faith + steps.
- Choose **faith over excuses**. (If you fight for your limitations, you get to keep them.)

**Declarations (say these):**

- I'm a **steward**, not just a consumer.
- **Income follows assets -** and I'm building assets.
- God opens my eyes to **hidden value**.
- I will not just survive; I will **thrive** and bless others.

**The Ability Test**

(Matthew 25:15) God gives resources **according to our ability**.
That means God's financial trust in you is directly tied to your **capacity to handle what He gives you**.

If you can't manage $10,000, you won't manage $100,000.
If you mismanage $100,000, **you won't be trusted** with $1,000,000.

**Your ability** is not just about **education**, titles, or charisma, it's also about your **discipline, priorities, and decision-making.**

**Generational Stewardship**

**"A good man leaves an inheritance to his children's children..."**
– (Proverbs 13:22)

Managing the 90% is about thinking beyond today's bills and this year's vacations. It's about thinking two, three, even four generations ahead.

**True Kingdom wealth:**

- Builds a financial foundation that supports ministry, missions, and community impact.
- Passes down wisdom along with wealth.
- Creates systems that outlast the steward.

---

**The Owner's Mindset (with Real Story)**

**While on a business trip to Kona, Hawaii.** I'm on a deck watching a gentle breeze blowing through the trees, and a simple truth hits me: **most of us hear a powerful word on Sunday and never turn it into a plan of action on Monday. Let's fix that – together.**

These next few pages is a straight-talk bridging from inspiration to implementation - told through true stories you've already heard me share – now organized as a blueprint you can use.

---

**The Question That Changes Everything**

When a habit, purchase, business idea, or relationship pattern isn't working, ask:
**"How's that working for you?"**
**If the answer is "not great," stop digging. Adjust the plan. Try the other side of the boat.**

**Church as a Strategy Lab (Not Just a Pep Rally)**

**We love good preaching. Assessment/Action:**

- Old mode: Information + inspiration → feelings.
- New mode: Information + inspiration → a written strategy for immediate implementation.

**Every time you receive a word, translate it into a week's worth of steps. Heaven provides seed; you till the soil.**

---

**Story 1 – "The Empty Lot That Started Paying Me"**

**Problem: I owned a rural half-acre lot that was costing me taxes and grass-cutting– no income, no plan.**

**Whisper: "Put a trailer on it."** I'd never owned a trailer. Still, I ran the numbers:

- Purchase a clean used 3-bed/2-bath single-wide trailer at a fair price
- Transport + set-up + tie-downs
- Connect power / water / sewer (neighbors had service; the lines just needed to reach my parcel)
- Basic cosmetics and safety checks
- Rent comps in the area

**Outcome: The numbers penciled. I moved the home onto the lot, connected utilities, and started collecting rent within a month. That "empty" dirt turned into a cash-flowing asset – and today it's free and clear and still paying, month after month.**

**Owner Steps**

- Walk the parcel. Confirm easements, access, zoning for manufactured housing.
- Call utility providers. Get written estimates to extend service to your property.
- Price transport/set-up with a reputable mover. (Get two quotes.)
- Pull rent comps. Demand that rents cover payment, taxes, insurance, maintenance, plus reserves.
- Close, set, connect, inspect, and list.

**Lesson: Land that perks (drain field) can be turned into land that pays you – if you'll see what others don't and act.**

**Story 2 – "Sneakers vs. Shares: The Nike Conversation"**

**Own enough shares in the company, and the dividends can buy your shoes. Now your assets pay for your liabilities."**

**Owner Steps**

- Open a low-fee brokerage account with DRIP (dividend reinvestment) turned on.
- Start small, automatic buys ($25–$50/week).
- Every time you "want" a brand, ask: *Do I own the company that makes it?*

**Mindset Shift: From consumer to owner.**

### Story 3 – "House Hacking: One Mortgage, Two Roommates"

My granddaughter bought a 3-bed/2-bath. She lived in one room and rented the other two. Those rents covered the whole mortgage. Now she's saving for property #2.

**Starter House-Hack Play**

- Target 3–4 bed homes near hospitals, campuses, or job centers.
- Add a lockable owner closet; set clear house rules in writing.
- Price rooms at market. Include utilities + Wi-Fi in rent.

**Result: You live almost free while building equity and landlord experience.**

---

### Story 4 – "From a 500 Credit Score to Keys in Hand"

**My daughter wanted to buy. Here's what worked:**

1. Pull credit and list fixes.
2. Open two small, secured loans/credit lines; pay on time for six months.
3. Join a credit union; ask for a road map to pre-approval.
4. We walked neighborhoods. I pray this prayer all the time:

**"Lord, show me what You want me to see - even what others can't."**
I spotted a small For Sale By Owner sign most people missed.

We negotiated the price below market. She closed. Her payment is lower than local rents - and **she's sitting on six-figure equity today.**

**Owner Steps**

- Build a payment track record (on-time, every time).
- Get pre-approved.
- Drive for deals each week. Call For sale by owner (FSBO) signs. Don't be shy, knock on the door.
- Ask: *What's the least you'd take if we can close quickly?*

---

**Story 5 – "Landlord Eyes: The Litter Box Lesson"**

One tenant insisted she had only a small dog with an "emotional support" letter. Red flags: long delays answering the door; "Don't go in that room."

A plumbing issue required access behind a bedroom panel. I looked - there was a litter box under the bed. I took photos on two separate visits. In court, the judge saw the evidence and granted the eviction for lease violations.

**Protect Your Investment**

- Record: photos, dates, communications. **Facts win.**

**Tie-in: Seeing what others can't see isn't just for acquisitions - it protects what you already own.**

---

**Bible Patterns You Can Build With**

**Jesus Borrowed a Boat (Luke 5)**

He turned Peter's fishing boat into a platform. Then He gave him divine direction: "Cast your net on the other side." Result? Overflow of fish that blessed other boats too.

**Owner Step**

- **Ask daily: *"Lord, which direction (side of the boat) today?"* Then obey now, not "when it feels right."**

---

**Leverage: One House or Five?**

**You have $100,000 to invest.**

- Plan A: Pay cash for one $100k rental.
- Plan B: Use 20% down and buy five $100k rentals with fixed-rate loans. Rent covers payments + reserves.

**When prices rose ~20% in hot years, five houses captured five times the appreciation. When rates climb (like now), be cautious:**

**Guardrails**

- Favor fixed rates.
- Stress-test: Could you survive a 10–15% rent dip?
- Keep reserves.
- Buy cash flow first, appreciation second.

---

**Compounding, But Simple**

**Compounding is interest on interest - a snowball rolling downhill.**

Copy This

- Automate a weekly or biweekly transfer into a broad index fund.
- Don't stop buying during dips in the market; you're buying more shares at lower prices (dollar-cost averaging).
- Think in decades, not days.

---

**"40 Acres and a Mule," Reimagined**

**For our grandparents, a mule was the work engine. Today, your "mule" might be:**

- A paid-off duplex

- A work truck for your business
- A dividend portfolio that pays your utilities
- A rental that covers your car note

**And the "40 acres"? Try 40 doors over time.**

**Legacy Play**

- One home per child (or grandchild) as the target.
- Keep a Legacy Binder: deeds, insurance, passwords, bank/LLC info, "Who to call" page.
- Put assets in the right entities; create clear transfer plans (Family Trust) to avoid family fights/probate.

---

### Marketplace Ministry Is Ministry

Jesus does miracles in boardrooms, job sites, title offices, and construction yards too. We don't separate "church" from "work." One Kingdom.

**Sunday → Saturday Translator**

- Sunday word: "Cast the net on the other side."
- Monday plan: Make 3 offers this week in your buy box.

**People tend to value what they pay for. Invest in your education, books, classes - and then act. Free wisdom is a gift; faith without works is dead.**

---

### The S-I-I Plan (Seed → Immediate → Incremental)

**1) Seed (Today)**

- Write one clear target: "Buy a cash-flowing duplex in 12 months."
- Define your buy box (zip codes, price, minimum cash-on-cash).

**2) Immediate (This Week)**

- Turn on auto-investing ($50–$200 per paycheck).
- Pull your credit report; write the fix list (utilization ↓, on-time payments ↑).
- Walk 3 properties; run numbers on 10; call 2 sellers.
- Join a real estate investor meetup or online group.
- Set landlord systems (application, screening, lease, move-in checklist).

**3) Incremental (Next 90 Days)**

- Put away 3 months' reserves per property you plan to own.
- Underwrite 20–30 deals; make 5–10 offers.
- Line up your team: lender, agent, attorney/closing, inspector, handyman.
- Practice this prayer on every drive:

**"Lord, show me what You want me to see - even what others can't."**

---

**Quick Scripts You Can Use**

**Calling a FSBO:**
"Hi, I saw your sign on [street]. I'm a serious buyer. If we kept this simple and closed on your timeline, what's the least you'd take?"

**Talking to a lender:**
"I'm targeting a small multifamily in the $X range. What credit, reserves, and documents do you need to pre-approve me this month?"

**Screening a tenant:**
"Here's our process: application, income verification, landlord references, and credit/eviction history. We follow it the same way for everyone."

### Health Fuels Wealth

**The wealthy protect their energy like they protect capital.**

- Move your body 3–4x/week.
- Protect sleep. Guard your mind.
- Clean (food) fuel most days.
- When you feel better, you communicate better – and communication is a wealth level all by itself.

---

### Owner Declarations

- I steward the 90% with wisdom and purpose.
- My money is disciplined, deployed, and working while I sleep.
- I am an owner; my assets pay for my liabilities.
- I hear the Holy Spirit; I see what others don't.
- I turn Sunday's revelation into Monday's plan.
- The Resurrection Power of Jesus Christ is at work in me now.

---

### Field Notes: What These Stories Prove

- Trailer on a lot: Assets can be created, not just bought.
- Nike dividends: Own what you love; let assets buy toys.
- House hacking: Live cheap; learn fast; scale.
- Credit → keys: Systems beat feelings.
- Litter box case: Verify. Document. Protect the asset.
- Leverage: Can multiply wins - only when paired with wisdom and discipline.
- Compounding: Tiny, steady moves become mountains.

- Vision of 40 rentals: Legacy is designed, not hoped for.
- Marketplace calling: Your work is worship.

---

**Your Monday Move (Do This Today)**

1. Write your buy box on paper.
2. Set an auto-invest (even $25).
3. Drive one target neighborhood and pray the seeing prayer.
4. Call one owner/agent and say the FSBO script.
5. Put your first three reserves deposits on the calendar.

**You don't need permission. You already have a word and a way. Now you have stories and steps. Let's go from pew to plan - then from plan to property - then from property to portfolio.**

**Managing the 90% laid the foundation – discipline**, stewardship, and maximizing what God already placed in your hand. But foundations are meant to be built upon.

**Now it's time to put that stewardship into action. Real estate is one of the most powerful plays in wealth-building because it combines cash flow, appreciation, leverage, and legacy in one arena. This is where theory meets practice.**

**If you've ever felt stuck living paycheck to paycheck, wondering how to break free, the answer is simple: run the play.**

**Welcome to Chapter 5 – Real Estate Power Plays.**

# Chapter 5

## **Real Estate Power Plays:** Tired of Living Paycheck to Paycheck? Just Run the Play

**Let me drop something on you:** You were created in the very image and likeness of God. That means you were designed with dominion – authority over the earth. Not just spiritually, but practically: **land**, resources, cattle, businesses, and **yes – real estate**. Dominion means the right to control, manage, and steward what God has placed in your hands.

**And here's the kicker:** ownership matters. **Real estate** is more than just a house or a building – it's **the surface of the land, the minerals underneath, the water running through it, and even the air space above it (that's why I love real estate)**. Owning real estate and other income-producing assets expands your influence, your options, and your legacy.

From the very beginning, God modeled creation. He spoke, He built, He formed. And because you're made in His image, you've been given that same ability to create - **buildings, books, music, businesses, art, inventions – that's in you**. (Jeremiah 1:5) reminds us: *"Before I formed thee in the belly I knew thee; and before thou camest forth out of the womb I sanctified thee, and I ordained thee a prophet unto the nations."*

So, **the real question is:** What has God set you apart and appointed you to do?

Because when you get this mindset – when you mix purpose with skillsets – you'll realize money isn't the goal. It's a tool. A tool that, when mastered, will serve your vision, fuel your investments, and advance the Kingdom.

**(Psalm 50:10) says it plain:** *"For every beast of the forest is mine, and the cattle upon a thousand hills."* Don't miss that part about Him owning 1000 hills **(He actually - owns all the hills)**. If God owns it all, and you are His child, then He's given you the right to steward, manage, and expand what He places in your hands. God has made you the head, and not the tail, above and not beneath. You are here to reflect who He is on the earth. Run the play (we'll talk about that later).

**Pearls of Wisdom by Dr. Leon**

**1. Make your money when you buy.**
The real profit in real estate is locked in at the purchase. If you buy right – below market value, in the right location, with the right potential – everything else that follows is simply icing on the cake. A great deal upfront creates a margin of safety and a foundation for wealth. Bad buys (overpaying) are very hard to "fix" later, but a great buy will bless you for years.

**2. I'm a buy–renovate–rent–and–hold guy.**
My philosophy is simple: Cash flow is king. Appreciation is wonderful, but it's the steady, predictable monthly income that frees you from the paycheck-to-paycheck grind. Renovate smartly – not lavishly – so the property commands higher rent and attracts quality tenants. Then hold it long-term, letting your tenants pay down the mortgage while your equity & cash flow grows, and don't forget the tax benefits.

**3. Consistency + Discipline = Millionaire Status.**
You don't need to flip 50 houses a year or hit the lottery to build real wealth. Educate yourself and improve your skillset. Work with a mentor who's weathered multiple real estate cycles – especially the 2008 – 2009 downturn. Keep cash or credit reserves ready so you can strike when fear grips the market and "there's blood in the streets."

When others panic, you'll be prepared, informed, and able to see opportunity. These are the seasons when millionaires are made.

Play the long game: stay focused, reinvest your profits, and resist shiny distractions. You can quietly hit millionaire status in under 10 years – without chasing fame or burning out. In real estate, the patient and disciplined win big.

**4. One property, many streams.**
The wealthy understand that one asset can have multiple income channels. A single property can pay you through:

- Monthly cash flow (tenants paying rent)
- Tax advantages (deductions, depreciation)
- Equity pay-down (loan balance shrinking every month)
- Appreciation (property value rising over time)
- Strategic leverage (use one property to buy the next)

**The key is to see beyond the front door – see the streams of wealth hiding inside.**

**5. Real estate is flexible.**
It's one of the few investments that lets you pivot when the market shifts. You can live in it, rent it, sell it, exchange it, owner finance it, or 1031 it into a bigger deal – all depending on your goals. The exit strategies are endless, which is why real estate is a **wealth tool** the wealthy never stop using.

**6. Get your spouse or partner's buy-in early.**
This isn't just an investment – it's a shared vision. You're building a future together, so alignment is everything. There will be seasons of sacrifice, late nights, and unexpected repairs, but when your partner is on board, you move in unity.

**7. Queen Status.**
When I first started, I asked my wife, *"What if we lose everything?"* She didn't flinch. She said, ***"We still have each other."*** That's more than support, that's LOVE, that's commitment, that's a friend, that's partnership, loyalty, faith and belief. When you have that kind of LOVE, favor, unity and trust, you can **move differently**. You take bigger, wiser risks because you know your foundation is unshakable.

### 8. Temperament to Be a Real Estate Investor

You must have the right mindset, emotional stability, and decision-making discipline required to succeed in real estate over the long term.

A successful investor's temperament includes:

- Patience – Understanding that wealth in real estate is built over years, not days.
- Resilience – Staying calm and solution-focused when deals fall through, tenants cause issues, or markets shift.
- Discipline – Sticking to your investment criteria and avoiding impulsive decisions.
- Adaptability – Adjusting strategies when economic or market conditions change.
- Emotional Detachment – Treating properties like business assets, not personal trophies.
- Compassion with Boundaries – Real estate is a **business** and a **tool God uses to care for you and your family**. You set expectations up front so everyone knows the standard. Then you follow through. Make the criteria clear at the beginning – then enforcement isn't personal later. If someone chooses not to honor the agreement, **they're not being "evicted by you" – they're evicting themselves** by stepping outside the boundaries they agreed to. Offer help without abandoning stewardship: point them to local agencies, churches, and assistance programs. Pray with them if they're open and still act quickly and consistently. Stay respectful and steward the asset God entrusted to you.
- Risk Awareness – Calculating risks realistically and not letting greed or fear drive decisions.

**Bottom Line:** The right temperament lets you weather market storms, avoid costly mistakes, and keep building your portfolio steadily – even when the headlines scream chaos.

## Real Estate Investing Terms – Made Simple

### Wholesaling

Finding a great deal on a property, putting it under contract, and then selling that contract to another buyer for a fee – without actually buying the property yourself. You're basically the "middleman" who connects sellers with investors.

### Pre-Foreclosures

Properties where the owner has fallen behind on their mortgage, but the bank hasn't taken it back yet. Often, owners are motivated to sell quickly to avoid foreclosure.

### Short Sales

When a property is sold for less than the amount owed on the mortgage, with the lender's permission. This often happens when the owner can't keep up with payments, but the bank would rather take a partial loss than foreclose.

### Foreclosures

Properties the bank has taken back because the owner didn't pay the mortgage. These are often sold at auction or directly by the bank (REO properties).

### Tax Deeds

When a property is sold by the county because the owner didn't pay property taxes. The buyer gets full ownership (a deed) after the sale.

### Due diligence

This is the investigation that is done before you buy the property **(get the property under contract 1st)**. Reviewing financials, inspecting the property, checking title(s), and making sure you understand every risk and opportunity. Due diligence protects you from costly surprises and bad investments (you must know what you're buying).

**Rehabs**
Properties that need repairs or updates. Investors buy them, fix them up, and either rent them out or sell them for a profit (fix and flip).

**Traditional Purchase**
Buying a property the normal way – with a mortgage from a bank, a down payment, and a closing process.

**Buy and Hold**
Buying a property and keeping it for a long time to make money from rent, property value increases, and tax benefits.

**Creative Finance**
Using non-traditional ways to buy property, such as owner financing, lease options, subject-to deals, or combining multiple financing sources.

**Self-directed IRA for real estate**

This is the term used for buying real estate inside an IRA (simply called a Real Estate IRA).

**Tax Lien Certificates**
When you pay someone's unpaid property taxes to the county, and in return, you get the right to collect that debt - with interest - from the property owner. If they don't pay, you may be able to take ownership.

**Owner Financing**
When the seller acts like the bank, letting you pay for the property in installments instead of getting a traditional mortgage.

**Combination Financing**
Using more than one funding source for a deal – for example, part bank loan, part private money, part your own cash.

**Bank Financing**
Getting a loan from a traditional bank or credit union to buy a property.

**Private Money Financing**
Borrowing from an individual (not a bank) who lends money in exchange for interest, often backed by the property.

**Hard Money Financing**
Short-term, high-interest loans from private lenders (or companies) that are based more on the property's value than your credit score. Common for flips and fast closings.

**Syndications**
When multiple investors pool their money together to buy a large property, such as an apartment complex, with profits shared based on each investor's contribution.

**Scout or Bird-Dog** – In real estate, a scout (or bird-dog) is someone who identifies potential property deals and refers them to an investor in exchange for a referral fee. They don't purchase or manage the property themselves – their value is in spotting opportunities early and connecting them to the right buyer. ***This role is ideal for new investors who are just getting started with little to no money, as it allows them to learn the business and earn while building connections.***

**Notes**
A note is a legal document that says someone owes a debt (like a mortgage or loan) and promises to pay it back. You can buy and sell notes just like you can buy and sell property.

**After Repair Value (ARV)**
An estimate of what a property will be worth after all repairs and renovations are completed. ARV helps investors decide how much to pay for a property and plan their profit margins.

**The BRRRR Method**

In real estate, there are a lot of strategies designed to maximize returns and build long-term wealth. One of the most popular in recent years is what many investors call the BRRRR® Method – a term popularized and trademarked by BiggerPockets.

BRRRR stands for Buy, Rehab, Rent, Refinance, Repeat. It's a systematic approach that allows you to recycle your capital, scale faster, and grow a portfolio without constantly needing fresh cash for every deal.

**Here's how it works:**

1. **Buy** – Find a property, usually undervalued or distressed, that you can pick up at a good price.
2. **Rehab** – Improve it. Renovate strategically to increase value, focusing on upgrades that matter to renters and appraisers.
3. **Rent** – Place quality tenants so the property generates stable cash flow.
4. **Refinance** – Once the property value has increased, refinance with a bank. Pull out some (or even all) of your original investment.
5. **Repeat** – Take that capital and do it again on the next property.

The beauty of this approach is that it turns one deal into the fuel for the next. Instead of parking your money in a single property forever, you put it to work again and again – multiplying your portfolio over time.

**Think of it this way:** BRRRR is not just about acquiring real estate, it's about creating a repeatable wealth-building system. **With the right mindset, skillset, and discipline, this strategy can literally change the trajectory of your financial future.**

**This guide:** walks you through each step of the process, explains key considerations, and offer insights on how to use this method to build your own real estate empire.

**Step 1: Buy**

The journey begins with the acquisition of a property that has untapped potential.

- What to Look For: Investors focus on distressed or undervalued properties – homes that need work, have been neglected, or are priced below market value due to their condition.
- Due Diligence: Before purchasing, perform a thorough analysis. This includes inspecting the property, estimating repair costs, researching local market values, and forecasting after-repair value (ARV).
- Financing: Many real estate practitioners use cash, hard money loans, or private money to acquire property quickly, as traditional lenders may hesitate to fund distressed assets.

**Step 2: Rehab**

Transform the property to maximize its value and rental appeal.

- Renovation: The rehab phase involves making necessary repairs and updates. This could range from fixing structural issues and updating plumbing or electrical systems, to cosmetic improvements such as painting, flooring, or landscaping.
- Budget and Timeline: Successful investors meticulously plan their renovations, balancing quality work with cost efficiency. Keeping projects on schedule and within budget is crucial to controlling expenses and maximizing profit.
- Value-Add: Focus on improvements that boost the property's market value and rental desirability – modern kitchens and bathrooms, open floor plans, and energy-efficient upgrades.

**Step 3: Rent**

Generate consistent income by finding reliable tenants.

- Tenant Selection: Once the property is rehabbed and ready, market it to potential renters. Screen tenants carefully to ensure timely payments and property care.

- Lease Terms: Establish clear, fair lease agreements. Consider the local rental market and set competitive rates that reflect the upgraded condition of the property.
- Property Management: Decide whether to manage the property yourself or hire a professional property manager. Effective management ensures steady cash flow and preserves the value of your investment.

**Step 4: Refinance**

Recapture your investment by leveraging the increased property value.

- Appraisal: After renting, seek a new appraisal to determine the property's post-rehab value. Ideally, the ARV will be significantly higher than the initial purchase price plus rehab costs.
- Loan Application: Apply for a long-term mortgage or cash-out refinance based on the updated value. Lenders typically require that the property be stabilized (rented) and in good condition.
- Capital Recovery: The goal is to pull out as much of your original investment as possible. If done correctly, you can recover the cash used to buy and rehab, which can now be used for your next deal.
- Debt Restructuring: Refinancing usually results in a lower-interest, longer-term loan, improving cash flow and freeing up capital for future investments.

**Step 5: Repeat**

Scale your portfolio by repeating the process.

- Portfolio Growth: With most or all of your initial capital returned, you can purchase another property and begin the cycle anew.
- Systems and Scaling: As you repeat the BRRRR method, develop efficient systems for sourcing deals, managing renovations, and handling tenants. This enables you to expand your holdings more rapidly and with less effort over time.

- Long-Term Wealth: The compounding effect of owning multiple cash-flowing properties, each purchased with recycled capital, can dramatically increase net worth and financial freedom.

### Why the BRRRR Method Works

This strategy leverages the power of forced appreciation – the ability to increase a property's value through targeted renovations. By refinancing after stabilization, investors can recycle their cash, reduce reliance on new capital, and accelerate portfolio growth. It's especially effective in markets where distressed properties are available and rental demand is strong.

### Risks and Challenges

- Renovation Overruns: Unexpected repairs or delays can eat into profits and hamper refinancing efforts.
- Appraisal Gaps: If the property doesn't appraise as high as expected, you may not recover all your invested capital.
- Vacancy: Difficulty finding tenants can disrupt cash flow and slow down the process.
- Lending Standards: Not all lenders are familiar with BRRRR or willing to refinance newly rehabbed properties quickly (**key factor in this current market**).

Mitigating these risks requires careful planning, conservative budgeting, and a reliable network of contractors and professionals.

### Case Study: BRRRR in Action

Let's consider a typical scenario:

- Purchase Price: $100,000 for a neglected single-family home.
- Rehab Costs: $40,000 to fully renovate.
- Total Investment: $140,000.
- After Repair Value (ARV): $200,000, as determined by market comparables.
- Rent: The upgraded home easily rents for $1,500/month.

- Refinance: The bank appraises at $200,000 and offers a loan of 75% LTV ($150,000). You pay back your initial investment and have $10,000 left over, plus monthly cash flow from rent.
- Repeat: Use recovered funds to purchase your next property, building a portfolio step-by-step.
- **Note:** The Total Investment of $140,000 does not reflect closings costs to buy and to refinance the property (know your numbers).

**Frequently Asked Questions**

- Can BRRRR work in expensive markets?
- It's most successful in areas with affordable distressed properties and strong rental demand. In high-priced markets, returns may be slimmer and refinancing more challenging.

**Do I need cash for the first purchase?**

Many use hard money or private loans to buy initially, then refinance with a conventional mortgage later.

How long does the BRRRR cycle take?

Timeframes vary; typically, the process takes several months from purchase through refinance.

**The Take-away**

The BRRRR method is a powerful blueprint for building wealth and scaling a real estate portfolio. By mastering each step– buying undervalued properties, renovating wisely, securing quality tenants, refinancing to recapture capital, and repeating the process– investors can accelerate growth and achieve financial independence. As with any investment strategy, success in BRRRR requires diligence, patience, and adaptability, but the rewards can be substantial for those who commit to learning and executing the method. **Bottom-line, it's just another tool in the toolbox**.

---

## The McCray 50/30 Strategy – Your Crisis-Proof Real Estate Game Plan

The McCray 50/30 Strategy was born out of hard lessons learned during economic storms – the kind that can wipe out years of progress if you're not prepared. It's more than a ratio; it's a philosophy for building, protecting, and preserving wealth in real estate no matter what the market does.

**It has two pillars:**

1. Equity Protection (50%)
2. Income Cushion (30%)

Both must work together if you want to thrive when others are in survival mode.

### Pillar 1 – Equity Protection (50%)

Your equity is your safety net. Without it, you're one bad market swing away from disaster.

Definition:
Maintain at least a 50% equity position across your entire portfolio. This means:

- Some properties may have 70% equity.
- Some may have 20–30% equity.
- Some may be fully paid off and generating 100% equity.
- But overall, if you added up all your debt and compared it to the total market value of your properties, you'd owe no more than half of what they're worth.

**Why It Matters:**

- Equity protects you from market downturns.
- Equity allows you to refinance, sell, or leverage without desperation.
- Equity attracts lenders and investors – they know you have skin in the game.

**How to Build & Maintain It:**

- Make aggressive principal payments when possible (especially in the early years of a loan).
- Reinvest part of your cash flow into debt reduction.
- Avoid overleveraging, even when lenders tempt you with "cheap" money.
- Monitor your portfolio's loan-to-value (LTV) twice a year.
- Keep select properties debt-free to act as *financial anchors* in your portfolio.

---

**Pillar 2 – Income Cushion (30%)**

Cash flow is the lifeblood of your portfolio. **Without it, you can be "asset rich" and still go broke**.

Definition:
Your total rental income should be able to take a 30% hit (from vacancies, rent reductions, or economic downturns) and still cover:

- All mortgage payments
- Taxes & insurance
- Utilities (if you pay them)
- Maintenance & repairs
- Management costs

**Why It Matters:**

- Economic downturns hit cash flow first, not equity.
- Vacancy spikes can cripple landlords who run too tight.
- A healthy cushion means you don't have to fire-sell properties in a panic.

**How to Build & Maintain It:**

- Set rents strategically – don't be the cheapest, but don't price yourself out of demand.
- Keep vacancy rates low through excellent tenant screening and retention.
- Maintain reserve accounts for each property (minimum 3–6 months of expenses).
- Perform bi-annual stress tests on your portfolio.

---

**Bi-Annual 50/30 Portfolio Stress Test**

Do this at least twice a year (more if warranted):

1. Calculate Total Equity:
   - Find the current market value of all properties.
   - Subtract the total debt owed.
   - Divide equity by total value to get your equity percentage.
   - Remember to include *fully paid-off* properties – they'll help your overall equity position.
2. Calculate Income Cushion:
   - Add up your gross monthly rental income.
   - Reduce it by 30%.
   - Check if the reduced amount still covers all expenses.
3. Take Action If You Fail:
   - Pay down debt on low-equity properties.
   - Refinance to lower interest rates.
   - Increase reserves or cash flow.
   - Sell non-performing or high-risk properties.

---

**Mindset for the McCray 50/30 Strategy**

- **Discipline over Desire: Just because you *can* buy more property doesn't mean you should.**
- **Protection before Expansion: Secure your current position before reaching for more.**
- **Steady Beats Flashy: Wealth is built in decades, not weekends.**

---

**Why This Strategy Works**

When markets are hot, the McCray 50/30 strategy keeps you from overextending.
When markets crash, it keeps you from losing everything.
It's a long-game wealth preservation plan that allows you to sleep at night while still growing your portfolio.

*** **Bonus** *** How to recognize a downward shift in the Real Estate (RE) Market: **When the Banks tighten their lending standards (making it hard to get financing) and canceling/eliminating/freezing previously approved lines of credit is a huge red flag**. Act quickly to sure up your RE portfolio. **Note: If you wait until after the lines of credit are frozen or cancelled to make your adjustments, it's likely to late and you may be in trouble.**

---

**Real Estate Investing Quick Reference Guide**

*Key Terms, Strategies & Crisis-Proof Principles – Made Simple*

---

**Foundational Terms**

| Term | Simple Definition | Key Tip |
|---|---|---|
| Wholesaling | Lock up a property under contract and sell that contract to another buyer for a fee – without buying it yourself. | Focus on finding motivated sellers. |
| Pre-Foreclosures | Owners are behind on payments but haven't been foreclosed on yet. | Move fast – sellers are often eager to avoid foreclosure. |
| Short Sales | Sell for less than is owed, with lender approval. | Requires patience; banks can be slow to approve. |
| Foreclosures | Bank-owned properties, often sold at auction or as REO. | Inspect carefully – many are sold "as-is." |
| Tax Deeds | County sells the property for unpaid taxes; buyer gets ownership. | Research liens and property condition before bidding. |
| Tax Lien Certificates | Pay another's unpaid taxes and earn interest; may get property if they don't pay. | Know the redemption period rules in your state. |

| | | |
|---|---|---|
| Due Diligence | Research before buying – financials, inspections, title, risks. | Always get it under contract first, then inspect. |
| Rehabs | Fix up properties for resale or rent. | Budget for surprises – they're common. |
| Traditional Purchase | Buy with a mortgage, down payment, and closing process. | Shop for best rates and terms. |
| Buy & Hold | Buy and keep for rental income, appreciation, and tax benefits. | Great for long-term wealth. |
| Creative Finance | Non-traditional deals like seller financing, lease options, or subject-to. | Learn contract details to protect yourself. |
| Owner Financing | Seller becomes the bank; you pay them directly over time. | Negotiate interest and terms carefully. |
| Combination Financing | Use multiple funding sources in one deal. | Keep track of each lender's terms. |
| Bank Financing | Loan from a bank or credit union. | Strong credit helps secure better rates. |
| Private Money Financing | Loan from an individual (not a bank). | Build trust – these are relationship-based. |
| Hard Money Financing | Short-term, high-interest loans based on property value. | Best for flips and fast closings. |

| | | |
|---|---|---|
| Syndications | Multiple investors pool money to buy larger properties. | Vet the sponsor carefully. |
| Scout or Bird-Dog | Someone who identifies potential property deals and refers them to an investor for a referral fee.<br><br>They don't purchase or manage the property themselves – their value is in spotting opportunities early and connecting them to the right buyer. Ideal for new investors just getting started with little to no money. | Build strong relationships with active investors and sharpen your eye for deals. |
| Notes | Legal debt documents like mortgages – can be bought and sold. | Verify payment history before buying. |

| | | |
|---|---|---|
| **After Repair Value (ARV)** | **Estimated value after renovations.** | **Critical for calculating offers and profits.** |
| **Leverage** | **Using borrowed money to buy more or larger properties than you could with cash alone.** | **Benefit: Magnifies returns and allows faster portfolio growth. Shortcoming: Increases risk – debt payments continue even if rents drop.** |

---

**Popular Strategies**

**The BRRRR Method**

Buy → Rehab → Rent → Refinance → Repeat

Buy: Target undervalued or distressed properties.

Rehab: Renovate to boost value and rental appeal.

Rent: Secure quality tenants for stable cash flow.

Refinance: Pull out original capital after value increases.

Repeat: Reinvest recovered funds into the next deal.

**Why It Works:** Forces appreciation, recycles capital, and scales portfolios faster.
**Watch Out For:** Over-budget rehabs, low appraisals, or vacancies.

---

**The McCray 50/30 Strategy**

**Crisis-Proof Real Estate Game Plan**

**Purpose:** *To survive and thrive through market ups and downs.*

**Pillar 1 – Equity Protection (50%)**

---

**Maintain at least 50% equity across your entire portfolio.**

Avoid overleveraging – keep some properties completely debt-free.

When possible, aggressively reduce debt to strengthen your balance sheet.

---

**Pillar 2 – Income Cushion (30%)**

---

Ensure your cash flow can withstand a 30% drop in income and still cover all expenses.

Maintain reserves equal to 3–6 months of expenses per property.

Screen tenants thoroughly to reduce vacancy risk and payment defaults.

---

**Bi-Annual 50/30 Portfolio Stress Test**

Equity Check – Calculate your total equity percentage across the portfolio.

Income Shock Test – Reduce projected rental income by 30% and confirm that expenses are still covered.

**Adjust if Needed – If you fail the test, take action:**

**Pay down debt**

**Refinance for better terms**

**Increase reserves**

**Sell underperforming or high-risk assets**

---

**Mindset:** *Protection before expansion.* Remember – wealth is built in decades, not weekends.

---

## Quick Takeaways for New Investors

- Learn the terms so you can speak the language of deals.
- Pick 1–2 strategies and master them before branching out.
- Always keep reserves – cash flow is oxygen.
- Protect equity like your life depends on it – because in real estate, it does.

---

***** Use leverage wisely – it can be your greatest accelerator or your fastest downfall.**

---

## Meet Alex – From Tenant to Investor

As my real estate journey continued, I met a young man named Alex. He was renting one of my apartments and had only been in the United States a short time, working long hours at a turkey processing plant in our rural town.

For months, whenever I stopped by the building to collect rent or check on repairs, I'd notice Alex watching me. One day, he finally got the courage to approach me.

"I've never seen someone who looks like me own property like this," he said.
"Would you be willing to coach me? Maybe I can take you to lunch or dinner, and you can tell me how you got started?"

His sincerity struck me. I told him I'd be glad to share what I'd learned– after all, teaching others is part of my God-given purpose.

---

**Learning the Game**

We began meeting for lunch. I taught him the basics– how to build credit, how to save for a down payment, how to position himself to get a loan, and strategies like house hacking.

What I didn't realize at first was that Alex was already doing his own version of house hacking. Though I charged $650 a month for the apartment, he was subletting by the bed– two beds in each room, a couple of makeshift beds in the living room– charging each person $250 per month. He had essentially turned the apartment into a rooming house.

Because the tenants covered all utilities and Alex kept the place in good condition, I didn't have a problem with it. He was making money, and I was getting steady rent. Eventually, he asked if he could rent more units to do the same thing. I agreed, and soon he was leasing three of my six units– managing them, collecting rent, and running his own little business.

---

**Small Beginnings, Big Moves**

Alex worked hard – his regular shift at the plant, plus side jobs. He even bought a van to start a small transportation service. If you've ever been inside a turkey processing plant, you know the work is tough, messy, and low-paying– but he took all the overtime he could get.

Following my advice, he saved aggressively and fixed his credit. I guided him through buying his first home. Soon, he brought his mother and sister from his home country, and they also began working at the plant. His home became another version of a house hacking, with others contributing to the mortgage payoff.

**Leveling Up**

I told Alex that to buy bigger properties, he needed to show at least two years of documented income on his tax returns. This would position him for bank financing on multi-family properties. He followed the plan exactly and purchased his second house.

What impressed me most was his gratitude. He always called me *Pastor* and said,

"You've changed my life– and my family's life. I'm teaching my mom and sister the same strategies you taught me."

**The Payoff**

Years later, after I'd moved away, I called to see how he was doing. The news blew me away:

- He now owns three income-producing properties.
- His mother and sister each owned their own homes.
- He had left the turkey plant, earned his CDL, and bought a semi-truck.
- He now drives cross-country, building wealth while his properties produce passive income.

**Alex is proof that with a coach, a teachable spirit, and the willingness to *run the play*, small beginnings can lead to a transformed life.**

## Case Study: From Turkey Plant Worker to Multi-Property Owner – How Alex Ran the Plays

Alex wasn't born into wealth.
When I met him, he was a tenant renting one of my apartments, new to the U.S., and working long shifts at a turkey processing plant– a job most people wouldn't touch. But Alex had something you can't teach: hunger for a better life.

He noticed I owned the building and finally asked me how I got started in real estate. He'd never seen anyone who looked like him in that position before, and it intrigued him. One day, he invited me to lunch to learn more. That lunch turned into regular coaching sessions where I walked him through the exact steps to get started.

---

### Play #1: House Hack to Generate Cash Flow

Alex was already *accidentally* running a house hack.
He rented a two-bedroom apartment from me for $650/month, then sublet beds to friends at $250 each. By the time he filled every bed– including makeshift ones in the living room– his rent, utilities, and more were covered. The rest? Pure cash flow in his pocket.

### Play #2: Build Credit and Save for a Down Payment

I coached Alex on how to:

- Establish strong credit
- Save strategically from his wages and side hustles
- Keep meticulous records of his income for bank approvals

---

**Play #3: Leverage OPM (Other People's Money)**

Once his credit score and savings were in place, Alex bought his first home with a small down payment– financed by the bank, paid off by the rent from people living there.

---

**Play #4: Multiply Income Streams**

With steady income and discipline, Alex bought a van to start a transportation side business. The van income, overtime pay, and rental cash flow all worked together to accelerate his wealth-building.

---

**Play #5: Rinse and Repeat**

**Over time, Alex bought more rental units– three in total– and helped his mother and sister (who had moved to the U.S. and worked at the same plant) buy their own homes. He duplicated the strategies I taught him across multiple properties.**

---

**Play #6: Level Up & Expand**

Alex eventually left the turkey plant behind. Using his rental income as a foundation, he earned his CDL, bought a semi-truck, and began making serious money driving cross-country– all while his rentals kept paying him every month.

---

**The Result:**
Alex went from a low-paying, physically demanding job to a financially independent entrepreneur with multiple properties, multiple income streams, and a skill set that will serve his family for generations.

---

## Key Takeaway

Alex didn't win because he had the most money or the best connections – he won because he had a coach, a plan, and the discipline to run the plays exactly as taught.

---

## The Big Picture

Alex's story is powerful, but here's the bigger picture - what he did isn't unique to him. The wealthy have been using these exact strategies for decades. The difference is, they've mastered how to structure deals, minimize risk, and maximize returns so the game of money works in their favor.

**This is why the wealthy love real estate… and why you should too.**

---

## The Power of Recognizing Your Moment

Recognizing your moment rarely comes with sirens, bells, or whistles – it usually shows up quietly, disguised as opportunity. I remember being at a real estate auction when I overheard a conversation about a club lot going up for sale in a prime location, high on a hill with a beautiful view of the water. They were selling buildable lots for $50,000–$60,000 and club lots – which you couldn't build on – for around $10,000–$15,000. But this one caught my attention because it was sandwiched between two buildable lots. Risk versus reward - was this one of those moments? The bidding started at $10,000, and I jumped in. Before I knew it, I got caught up in the auctioneer's rhythm: "going once, going twice, sold!" I walked away with the lot for $35,000. Immediately I began to question myself: Had I broken my own rule of never overpaying? Had I let excitement override discipline? My max should have been $15,000. In real estate, you make your money when you buy, not when you sell – so had I violated my own principle?

But remember the conversation that I overheard, this lot was sandwiched between two buildable lots. That meant something to me. Shortly after I closed, the homeowner's association announced that some of the club lots would be converted into buildable lots. Two months later, I found out mine was one of them. Suddenly, that $35,000 purchase became a prime buildable lot. I put it back on the market and it sold for $80,000. What looked like a risky move became a Kingdom reminder: when you acknowledge God and move in faith, He can turn what feels like a mistake into a miracle. From $35,000 to $80,000 – that's the power of recognizing your moment. Praise Him.

---

If you've ever wondered why so many wealthy people have real estate somewhere in their portfolio, the answer is simple: it's the perfect blend of security, flexibility, and profitability.

**The wealthy understand a truth that most people overlook:** real estate is the great multiplier. It doesn't just grow your wealth – it accelerates it, protects it, and passes it on.

### 1. It's Tangible Wealth You Can Touch

Unlike stocks, bonds, or crypto, you can walk into a property you own. It's physical, real, and not subject to vanishing in a market crash overnight. The wealthy love assets they can see and control – especially ones that meet a basic human need: **shelter**.

---

### 2. Cash Flow That Doesn't Sleep

Real estate pays you whether you're working or sleeping. Tenants cover the mortgage, taxes, insurance, and still leave you a monthly profit. The wealthy use this steady cash flow to fund other investments, travel, or reinvest into more properties – compounding their income streams.

---

### 3. Built-In Tax Advantages

Tax benefits are one of the wealthiest investors' favorite secrets. Depreciation, expense write-offs, and tax-deferred exchanges allow them to keep more of their money working for them instead of giving it away to Uncle Sam. Every dollar saved in taxes is another dollar compounding for their future. This is a huge reason why many of the wealthy pay little to no federal taxes!

### 4. Appreciation and Equity Growth

While tenants are paying down the loan, the property is (historically) increasing in value. The wealthy think decades ahead – knowing that even small annual appreciation becomes massive over time when combined with loan pay-down.

---

### 5. Leverage is the Superpower

In real estate, you don't have to pay 100% of the purchase price to control 100% of the property. This is the power of leverage – the ability to use the bank's money or other people's money to control a high-value asset while investing a fraction of your own cash.

The wealthy understand that money is a tool, and the goal is to put as little of their own money into a deal as possible while maintaining strong equity and cash flow. This keeps their personal capital liquid and ready for the next opportunity or additional reserves as needed.

It's why you'll rarely see a seasoned investor pay full price in cash – just like you'll rarely see an airline buy an entire fleet with their own money, or a growing business expand without outside financing. They use OPM to scale portfolios at lightning speed, move on opportunities before competitors, and build wealth faster than they ever could by paying cash.

**Leverage, when used wisely**, isn't just a tactic – it's a force multiplier that turns ordinary investors into empire builders **(get trained and use it wisely)**.

---

**6. Multiple Exit Strategies**

The wealthy love that they can pivot depending on market conditions:

- Rent it out for income
- Flip it for profit
- Exchange it for a bigger property
- Owner-finance it for passive payments
- Redevelop it for higher returns

**They never feel "stuck" because real estate always offers options.**

---

**7. Legacy and Generational Wealth**

Real estate is more than a personal investment – it's a family strategy.

**A Story I've Seen Too Many Times**

I can't tell you how many times I've watched this play out in our communities – both in the inner city and out in the country. A family works hard their whole life, finally buys a home, and when they pass away, they leave that one house to their children. Sounds good, right? A blessing?

But here's the problem. Let's say you've got **four kids and only one house**. Now what?

One child says, ***"I want to live in it."*** Another says, ***"We should sell it and split the money."*** A third **doesn't care either way** but refuses to sign any paperwork. Meanwhile, **nobody's paying the property taxes or fixing the roof that's leaking**. Next thing you know, the family is fighting, the bills pile up, and **before long the house is lost** – not because they didn't love their parents, but because there was no plan.

I've seen too many families lose the very thing their parents sacrificed for. **The wealth is gone in one generation, and the cycle of struggle continues**.

---

### What Could've Been Different

Imagine if that same **family owned just one more house**. The first house is where they lived. The second? **A rental property**. That **rental income could cover taxes, maintenance, and even be divided fairly among the kids**. Over time, **that extra house could grow into two, three, four houses – one for each child, or even for the grandchildren**. That's how families start building **generational stability** instead of generational conflict.

And here's the beauty: rental properties don't just pay the bills. They come with tax advantages, and banks are far more willing to finance income-producing property if your credit and cash flow are lined up. The wealthy have known this for generations. **That's why Scripture says:**

***"A good man leaves an inheritance to his children's children."*** **(Proverbs 13:22)**

Notice it doesn't just say children – it says *children's children.* That means thinking beyond today and setting up a system where the next two, three, or four generations can thrive.

---

### The Hard Truth

Right now, homeownership in America is sitting at around 65.7%. But when you break it down, **it tells another story**:

- 73.8% of White families own homes.
- 63.0% of Asian families.
- 49.8% of Hispanic families.
- And only 45.9% of Black families.

"Only about **4–5% of housing units** in the U.S. are second homes, and an even smaller share of the total population owns multiple homes. Yet **these assets play a pivotal role in building generational wealth** – home **equity**

**remains a primary avenue for long-term wealth preservation and intergenerational transfer."**

From Census-based CPS/HVS data for the fourth quarter of 2023.

---

**The Call to Action**

So, here's my question to you: **How many children and grandchildren do you have?** And what do you want to leave them? Another fight over one house – or a foundation they can build on?

This isn't about greed. It's about legacy. It's about seeing real estate not just as "my house," but as a strategy – a **Kingdom strategy – for the future**. One more house, purchased with wisdom, with a plan, and with the guidance of the King of Kings, can literally change your family tree.

I've watched too many families lose it all. **I don't want that for you**. Build with a goal. Build with a plan. And above all, **invite God into the process** – because legacy without Him is just property. But **legacy with Him becomes inheritance, stability, and a testimony of His faithfulness for generations to come**. ***This is a key to Unlock the "Wealth Code" (Run the Plan)***.

---

**8. It's a Hedge Against Inflation**

When prices rise, so do rents and property values. The wealthy use real estate as a shield against the erosion of their money's buying power. While others are losing value, their assets are keeping pace – or even outpacing inflation.

---

**Here's the bottom line:**
The wealthy don't just "like" real estate – they use it as a financial foundation, a cash-flow machine, a tax shelter, a legacy builder, and a safety net all in one. They know that once you understand the plays, you can win in any economy.

**And that's exactly what we're about to cover next – the plays the wealthy run over and over again to turn real estate into a lifelong wealth engine.**

### Play #1: Buy Below Market Value

Rule: You make your money when you buy, not when you sell.
Look for motivated sellers, distressed properties, or off-market deals. Use wholesalers, probate lists, pre-foreclosures, or direct-to-owner marketing. A property bought at 70–80% of its true value sets you up for instant equity.

### Play #2: Force Appreciation

Don't just wait for the market to go up – make it go up.
Strategic renovations (kitchen, baths, curb appeal, energy upgrades) can immediately raise property value and rental rates. Wealthy investors focus on *value-add plays* that create equity fast.

### Play #3: Maximize Cash Flow

Increase income and reduce expenses:

- Add laundry machines, parking fees, storage rentals, pet fees
- Implement RUBS (Ratio Utility Billing System) so tenants share utility costs
- Negotiate better rates on insurance and services
  The more net income you generate, the higher your property's value becomes.

### Play #4: Leverage Other People's Money (OPM)
Banks, private lenders, equity partners, hard money lenders – wealthy investors rarely rely solely on their own cash.

Why? Because using only your own money limits your reach. If you have $100,000 in capital and buy one property outright, you've tied up all your resources in a single deal. But if you leverage that same $100,000 as down payments or capital injections across multiple properties, you could control three or four assets instead of just one.

Think about it – very few people buy a home in cash. They take out a mortgage, pay a fraction of the cost upfront, and control 100% of the property. The same principle applies to a McDonald's franchise owner who uses bank financing to open multiple locations, an airline that finances multi-million-dollar planes, or even a church that uses a mortgage to build a sanctuary. In each case, OPM allows the organization or investor to control more, grow faster, and keep cash available for the next move.

*****Warning***** Using leverage via credit cards, consolidation loans, lines of credit or otherwise for buying non-income producing stuff that does not pay for itself **(bad debt)** is a trap by the enemy to ensnare you, steal from you and to destroy your future **(don't do it)**.

This is not about recklessly borrowing – it's about strategically aligning with funding sources that allow you to keep your money moving while their money works for you. **Get educated and use wisdom**.

**Play #5: Use Strategic Tax Moves**

- Depreciation: Deduct part of the property value each year
- 1031 Exchange: Sell a property and buy another without paying capital gains now
- Cost Segregation: Accelerate depreciation to shelter more income now The wealthy play the long game – keeping more money in the system to reinvest **(think like the wealthy and play the game too).**

### Play #6: Multiply Streams of Income

One property can pay you in multiple ways:

1. Monthly rent (cash flow)
2. Loan pay-down by tenants (equity)
3. Appreciation over time
4. Tax savings
5. Optional income from amenities, storage, parking, or creative leasing strategies

---

### Play #7: Recycle Capital

Refinance or do a cash-out once equity has grown, then redeploy those funds into the next property.
The wealthy keep their money in motion, never letting it sit idle. This is how they scale portfolios without constantly injecting fresh cash.

**Here's the key:**
The wealthy don't get rich from one lucky deal – they get rich by running these plays over-and-over, staying disciplined, and making decisions based on numbers, **not emotions**.

---

### Why the Wealthy Love Real Estate

Most people drive past opportunities every single day and never even notice them. They see "just another house," "just another building," or "just another piece of land." But the wealthy? They see cash flow, tax savings, leverage, and generational wealth wrapped in brick, mortar, and dirt.

Once you understand the game, it's like having the cheat-codes to the financial system. Real estate is more than an investment – it's the Swiss Army knife of wealth: shelter, income, tax protection, appreciation engine, leverage tool, and legacy builder all in one.

**That's why the wealthy never stop playing this game – and why it's time for you to learn the rules they live by.**

The wealthy know something the average person doesn't: real estate allows you to control big assets with small amounts of your own money – often using other people's money (banks, investors, even government programs).

**With the right moves, you can:**

- **Control** a property with minimal out-of-pocket cash.
- **Leverage** banks and investors to fund purchases.
- **Earn** from rent, appreciation, and tax benefits.
- **Pull cash out** tax-free through refinancing.

In short – it's like owning a machine that prints money… and the government helps you maintain it.

### Government Incentives – The "Secret Bonus Level"

The government actually *wants* you to own investment property because you're solving a housing and development problem for them. **In exchange, they offer powerful perks:**

- **Depreciation** – Write off the "wear and tear" of the property (on paper) **even if it's increasing in value**.
- **1031 Exchange** – Sell and buy a new property without paying capital gains taxes.
- **Tax-Free Refinancing** – Pull equity from your property without triggering a tax bill.

- **Expense Deductions** – Repairs, maintenance, travel, and management expenses can all be deducted.

These incentives are why real estate has built more millionaires than almost any other asset class.

---

### Assets vs. Liabilities – The Wealth Filter

It's simple:

- **Assets** put money in your pocket every month.
- **Liabilities** take money out.

The wealthy let their assets pay for their liabilities. Want a car or boat? Buy an income-producing property first and then let the cash flow from that property cover the payment. Now your luxury is paid for without touching your paycheck.

### The Hidden Land Story

Years ago, someone inherited an old, overgrown property in the middle of town – "Grandma's house" – vacant for 12 years and hidden under vines. It sold at auction for $135,000.

The new owner discovered the lot was 10.25 acres, not the 2.5 acres listed on old county records. They cleared the land, revealed a prime location, and suddenly the possibilities exploded:

- Luxury single-family home
- Upscale four-plex
- 100-unit apartment complex
- Strip mall
- Mixed-use high-rise

The value was always there. It just needed someone with vision to see it. That's the power of positioning and perspective in real estate.

## Cash Flow – The Magic Trick

Passive income from rental properties means you can be anywhere – even on a beach – while your bank account grows. The property works for you even when you're not working. The goal is to build enough monthly cash flow to pay for your life.

## The Manage-the-90% Rule

Tithing and giving is important because it honors God and demonstrates to Him that He can trust you. However, what you do with the **90%** is where wealth is built. Invest a portion of that 90% into assets that generate more income. Reinvest profits instead of inflating your lifestyle too quickly.

## Multiple Streams = Multiple Safety Nets

The wealthy don't rely on one paycheck. In real estate, multiple streams might mean:

- Long-term rentals
- Short-term/Airbnb rentals
- Commercial leases
- Storage, parking, laundry, or pet fees
- Forced appreciation through upgrades

If one stream slows down, others keep flowing.

## The Positioning Principle

Opportunities in real estate move fast. Being "in position" means you're ready to act:

1. **Know your market** – neighborhoods, trends, and price points.
2. **Be financially ready** – cash reserves, financing, or investor partnerships in place.

3. **Sharpen your skills** – learn to analyze deals quickly.
4. **Build your network** – stay connected to agents, lenders, contractors, and other investors.

When opportunity knocks, you don't have time to get ready – you must ***be* ready**.

**The Power of Seeing**

The best deals aren't always labeled "hot opportunity." They often look like problems: outdated buildings, vacant lots, or underused land. Successful investors have the ability to see what a property *could be* – not just what it is today.

**Hidden value can be found in:**

- Cosmetic or structural improvements.
- Land in the path of new development.
- Buildings that can be repurposed.
- Locations undervalued due to old perceptions.

**The Power of Listening**

- In real estate, vision matters – but listening can be your edge. The investors who win aren't just good at understanding the numbers; they're good at reading people. Sellers don't hand you the deal on paper – they hand it to you in their stories, their pauses, their worries, and the details they repeat without realizing it.
- I learned to listen to three channels at once:
- **What's said.** The facts: price, timeline, condition.
- **How it's said.** The emotion: urgency, frustration, pride, grief.
- **What isn't said.** The gaps: the decision-maker you haven't met, the tax bill they're dodging, the move-out date they keep skipping past.

- When you really hear a seller, you're not negotiating against them – you're keying into how you can solve their problem. When you find out the problem, figure out how to solve their problem while crafting a solution that meets your needs and their needs for a win-win solution. You'll find out that when their problem is solved, your contract writes itself.

**A Quick Story**

I was out on one of my driving-for-dollars loops near the house when a small, easy-to-miss "For Sale" sign caught my eye. I called, we met at McDonald's, and after a few questions…I just listened.

In my listening, I heard a man trying to hold his world together. He owned several properties, and a heavy tax bill was coming due, and he needed a fast, clean solution without paying commissions. As I continued to listen, I found out that he had cancer. More than anything, he wanted his family covered – not tangled up in debt or delays. I felt that. I stopped and prayed with him on the spot for supernatural healing. What he was really asking for was certainty that the deal would close speedily and at a fair price. We agreed on a number and a quick closing date.

I went home and wrote the contract that fit *him* and worked for me: fair price, **as-is**, quick close, no agents, clear net in his pocket. I called him within the hour, we met again, and we signed. His problem was solved, and I gained a solid cash-flowing asset that I still own today. I listened to the person behind the property, served his true need, and the deal wrote itself. **Listening** is a **"Wealth Code" Unlocked Solution**.

**Real Estate Power Plays**

Real estate is a wealth vehicle where:

- Banks give you money to buy it.
- Tenants pay it off for you.
- The government rewards you for owning it.

- And you can pass it down, so your children start ahead.

**Testimony of God's Goodness and Supernatural Favor:**

**Understanding the real estate game is more than just a path to wealth – it's about building lasting resilience and legacy.** Real estate isn't a sprint, it's a marathon. It's about playing the long game, keeping steady through the ups and downs, and knowing that storms will come but they don't have to sink you.

For a season, it seemed like everything I touched turned to gold. Deal after deal, win after win – the hand of God was so evident that even others noticed. I remember one day on a rehab project, my handyman stopped, looked at me, and said, *"The Lord must really love you."* Without hesitation I smiled and said, *"He does – and He loves you too."*

But don't be mistaken – it wasn't all smooth sailing. Like anyone else, I faced my share of real estate challenges. Yet every obstacle became a classroom, and through God's grace, I was given wisdom to solve problems, pivot strategies, and keep moving forward.

**Here's the truth:** the real estate world rewards those who can weather storms, adapt quickly, and keep their eyes fixed on what matters most. Celebrate the victories, yes – but never lose sight of the foundation beneath them. Behind every open door and every closed one is the same source: God Himself.

**Real estate is not a gamble – it's stewardship.** And when you recognize the true source of your success, you won't just build properties, you'll build purpose, stability, and Kingdom impact that lasts for generations. **"Wealth Code" Unlocked.**

**Check out this next play that you need to have in your toolbox:**

Speaking of tools in the toolbox…
What happens when the wins start stacking up, and you're giving God all the praise out loud – but deep down, in the quiet corners of your mind, you start thinking, *"Maybe it had a little something to do with my skills… my training… my insight?"*

That's when God has a way of reminding you – sometimes gently, sometimes not so gently – that it's always been Him. It always was. It always will be.

**So, here's the tool: never let success trick you into thinking you're the source. You're just the steward. Put that in your toolbox. "Wealth Code" Unlocked.**

---

**Nothing could prepare me for what was about to hit. Just as I was celebrating breakthroughs in one area, the entire financial world was collapsing in another.**

**From Breakthrough wins to Financial Earthquake:**

In 2008, the world as we knew it came crashing down. The real estate market collapsed, the stock market tanked, and the economy seemed to unravel overnight. Like millions of others, my family and I were hit hard. Our income dropped by more than 60%, and it felt like everything we had built was slipping through our hands.
Once a few payments were missed, the dominoes began to fall. Foreclosure notices started showing up, creditors began circling, and eventually, I faced what I once thought unimaginable: a $9 million setback. My credit score – once a healthy 720 – plummeted to 450.

I can still remember the feeling in those moments. The hurt, embarrassment. The weight of disappointment. The uncertainty of not knowing how we would make it through. It was a humbling, crushing season. We went through our savings, sold what we could, and did everything possible to keep our family afloat.

But somebody say, *But God.*

Through it all, we never missed a meal. We never went homeless. We never lost our cars or our home. Somehow, God always made a way. And no matter how bad things looked, I kept reminding myself: **"God is still on the Throne.** This didn't surprise Him. If He blessed me once, He can and will do it again."

---

**The Miracle of the VA Church Property**

One of the hardest battles during that time was over our community center and church building – the very place we worshiped God. The mortgage was $3,500 a month, far too much in those tight times. But the bank agreed to a forbearance, reducing it to $2,000 per month.

We paid that faithfully – for eight years. Yet, behind the scenes, the original balance continued to grow with fees and interest, ballooning to over $725,000. On paper, it looked impossible. Then, I got a call from the VP at the bank, calling me in to inform me that my time was winding up and the bank was at a decision point – you get it refinanced through another bank or the property would have to be taken back. A tough hit, but I knew Who I served. Later on I went back to the bank with a bold request: "If I can refinance and bring you $250,000 cash, will you release the note?" I believed in faith – and to my surprise, they agreed without any negotiation. That launched a long, painful journey of 12 bank rejections. Application after application was denied. Every door I tried seemed to slam shut. Finally, the bank gave me a deadline – either come up with the $250,000, or they would take the building back.

I prayed. I pressed. And then one night at a local real estate meeting, I met a bank manager. We talked, I submitted my application – and this time, it was approved.

Hallelujah! My heart overflowed with joy and gratitude. The original bank honored their word, released the $725,000 debt for the $250,000 payoff, and even agreed not to report the write-off as taxable income. That's nothing short of a miracle. I've seen the powerful Hand of God move time after time in my life – and I'm so very grateful. He favors me – which even now brings tear to my eyes. What a big and awesome God that we serve. *My God is....*

---

**Restoration**

Fast forward. Ten years after that crushing economic reset, my credit score is not only restored – it's stronger than ever, now over 800.

Even during this tough season, God's hand was upon me. But **the greatest testimony** - in this season while the banks had turned their backs on me, God raised up an unlikely ally. An elderly gentleman name Mr. David Jefferson, a man I had never met before, stepped into my life. For years, while banks wouldn't touch me, Mr. David Jefferson funded my real estate purchases.

God used him as a vessel to keep me moving forward in my calling and to prove that when one door closes, He can open another – often through someone you never expected.

---

**Final Thought**

The 2008 crash was devastating, humiliating and humbling. The journey was long and hard. But through it all, God was faithful. We never lost our residence, never lost our church, retained the 6-unit apartment building and more.

And here's what I've learned: **your lowest valley can become the foundation of your greatest comeback. Fast forward to today, and I'm so grateful to the King of Kings – restoration greater than before the storm. He's a big and awesome God.** No matter the storm, keep declaring: ***"God is still on the Throne."*** It's one of the biggest **"Wealth Code" Unlocked**. If He blessed you before, **He could do it again**.

**The Tampa Church Property**

*A True Story of Vision, Strategy, and God's Timing*

I've always dreamed of moving back to Florida – especially Tampa, where I grew up. My heart's been tied to the water since I was a kid hanging out at Clearwater Beach. Even after decades in the military, civil service, and running my own businesses during my time in Virginia, that dream never left me.

One cold Virginia winter, I asked my wife again, "Are you ready to move to Florida?" This time, she said, "Yes." Within days, I booked the movers, and we were - headed to Florida before she could change her mind. But check this out – about six months before that big move, there was **a divine appointment**.

**The Unexpected Find**

On a previous trip to check my Florida investments, I drove past a small church for sale. At first, I ignored it – I wasn't looking to start another ministry. But the next day, I felt prompted to take a closer look.

It was an older, 1960 sq. ft. building in a transitioning neighborhood – close to malls, Raymond James Stadium, the airport – but with only two parking spots, which scared buyers away. Asking price: $137,000.

Where others saw a problem, I saw possibilities. With the right plan, this could be a church, an office, or even a single-family home.

**The Creative Deal**

I knew churches are hard to finance through banks, so I asked for **seller financing**:

- **Purchase Price:** $137,000
- **Down Payment:** $30,000
- **Terms:** 3 years, interest-only at $356.67/month
- **Bonus:** The church rented it back for 12 months at $800/month

That meant I was **cash-flow positive from day one** – $443/month profit with no headaches.

### From Cash Flow to Construction

Year one was smooth. Then a second church leased for $1,200/month. More profit, more stability.

Then 7 months later, COVID hit. The tenants left, and I decided to pivot – turning the church into a **3-bed, 2.5-bath single-family home**. I even hired the former tenants, who were experienced builders, to do the remodel.

**The plan:**

- Full gut rehab down to concrete block walls
- All new plumbing, electrical, windows, HVAC, roof, and interiors
- Granite countertops, upgraded kitchen and bathrooms, open floor plan

---

### Surprises & Setbacks

Two big curveballs hit:

1. **$6,000 impact fees** from the city just for changing from a church to a home
2. **Hurricane window requirements** with reinforced steel installed in the walls – expensive and time-consuming

I'd budgeted for overruns, but these pushed me over. Still, we pressed on, financing the rehab with a hard-money loan.

---

### A Stunning Transformation

When it was done, the property looked brand spanking new. I'd expected it to be worth $300k – but the market had heated up. Then another factor came into play: my dream wasn't just to live in Florida. I wanted to live **by the water**.

**The Daytona Beach Shift**

On a trip to Daytona, we found a beautiful home **half a block from the ocean**. Coffee or tea on the porch with a water view (that works for me).

The decision was clear: sell the Tampa home, move to Daytona Beach.

**The Sale & the Blessing**

I listed the Tampa home expecting $300k. God had other plans – it sold for **$400,000**.

**The Numbers:**

- Purchase: $137,000
- Renovations: $110,000
- Total investment: $247,000
- Net check at closing: **$172,000 profit**

  **The tithe check was $17,200**. If you're having challenges giving God $250 from a $2,500 check, it would be almost impossible for you to wrap your brain around giving Him $17,200 out of $172,000 check. Let's be real – if God sees that you can't be faithful at the $2,500 level, can you really be trusted at the $172,000 level **(I'm just saying)**? Be faithful over the little and....

- Plus: Almost 2 years of tenants covering mortgage, utilities, and putting cash in my pocket

**Hidden in Plain Sight**

Neighbors told me they'd driven by for years and never noticed the building. God had kept it hidden until the right time.

**Lessons from This Deal**

1. **Always have multiple exit strategies** – church, office, home conversion **(check with your local zoning office)**.
2. **Creative financing beats traditional banks** for unique properties.
3. **Cash flow first** – your property should pay for itself.
4. **Be ready to pivot** – market changes and life goals matter.
5. **God's timing is perfect** – He'll reveal opportunities others can't see.

---

**In Chapter 5,** we broke down the **Real Estate Power Plays** – practical strategies that can move you out of the paycheck-to-paycheck cycle and into financial abundance. You saw that wealth isn't about luck or chance; it's about knowing the plays, running them with discipline, and refusing to stay stuck in survival mode.

**But here's the truth:** running plays will only take you so far, but now you must shift to a higher Kingdom Level of – "Seeing What Others Cannot See".

# Chapter 6 – Seeing What Others Cannot See

*Activating Visionary Insight for Wealth, Purpose, and Legacy*

There's a level of living, leading, and investing that requires more than natural sight – it requires what we'll call visionary insight. The ability to see what others overlook. To perceive value others miss. To hear opportunity where others hear noise.

And here's the truth: God wants to give you that vision.

**"Where there is no vision, the people perish..." (Proverbs 29:18, KJV)**

---

## Seeing What Others Cannot See

"One of the greatest keys to building wealth and advancing the Kingdom is the ability to see what others cannot see.
This isn't just about eyesight – it's about insight. It's about looking at the same world everyone else sees, but noticing patterns, opportunities, and shifts that others overlook."

- When you can anticipate where the world is heading, you can position yourself ahead of the curve.
- The average person reacts to change. The visionary prepares for it.
- Seeing ahead means you can make strategic moves before the masses catch on – whether in business, real estate, technology, or investments.
- This ability is part faith, part wisdom, and part strategy. It's a God-given advantage for those willing to pay attention.
- The kind of wealth and impact you're called to walk in cannot be reached with average sight. It requires a higher lens – and a different level of clarity.

- But here's the exciting part – God is not hiding things *from* you. He's hiding things *for* you.
- He delights in showing His children treasures hidden in plain sight – those who are willing to lean in, listen closely, and look again.
- "It is the glory of God to conceal a thing: but the honour of kings is to search out a matter." (Proverbs 25:2, KJV)
- God doesn't just bless you with things – He blesses you with the ability to see things.
- He gives Kingdom Sons and Kingdom Daughters a divine edge – the ability to look beyond the natural and discern what others walk past.
- Sometimes it's an idea that won't leave you alone. Other times it's a whisper that says, "Look again," when others say, "There's nothing there."
- There's a fire that ignites when you realize God wants to partner with your eyes – not just to see what is, but to glimpse what could be.

He's doing a divine "show & tell," but not for the masses. It's reserved for those who are sensitive, submitted, and serious about fulfilling their assignment. **For those who will say:**

- "Lord, show me what You see."
- "Let me walk through doors others are too afraid to knock on."
- "Use my life as a canvas to display Your vision."

**If you've ever wondered how some people seem to be "ahead of the curve," this is it: Visionary insight.**

They're not just guessing. They're seeing what's coming because they're tuned into a higher frequency. They've trained their spiritual eyes to see beyond the obvious.

That's why it's *fun*, exciting, and faith-building to be in this kind of flow. Every moment could become a Kingdom setup. Every piece of land, every conversation, every divine connection could unlock something incredible.

Vision fuels purpose. Vision inspires movement. Vision attracts favor.

Are you ready to ask God to anoint your eyes? Are you willing to step into this realm of revelation and receive downloads tailored just for you? Are you ready to see?

**Sensitivity to See**

When it comes to building wealth, walking in purpose, and leaving a legacy, one of the greatest prayers you can pray is to ask God for wisdom and the sensitivity to see what He wants you to see – especially the things hidden in plain sight that others miss. In (Genesis 21:14–19), Hagar found herself in a desperate situation. She was so focused on the problem that she could not see the solution right in front of her. **While she wept, her son Ishmael prayed**, and **God heard his cry**. Then the scripture says, *"God opened her eyes, and she saw a well of water."* The well was there all along, but her eyes had to be opened to see it. Many times, the provision, the opportunity, or the strategy you need is already within reach, but you can't access it until God sharpens your vision. So, let me ask you: **what are you not seeing right now that you need to see?**

**Reflection Moment**

Hagar was overwhelmed by her problem and missed the solution that was right in front of her until God opened her eyes. The well was there all along.

- What problem has been blinding you from seeing God's provision?
- What opportunities might already be within reach, waiting for your eyes to be opened?
- Take a moment to pray: *"Lord, open my eyes to see what You've already placed around me."*

---

**Let's check-out real-life examples where visionary insight created wealth, legacy, and impact – all because I chose to see what others couldn't.**

**Real Estate Deal:** The MLK Project (Seeing Past the Surface)

God often speaks through promptings. That day, I felt a pull to look at a particular commercial property. At first glance, it was ugly – a lot of work and too big of a project. But I felt compelled to look again.

On my second visit, I saw potential others couldn't see. It had been a college frat house and office space, listed for $95,000. Smaller homes nearby were selling for more. Multiple exit strategies revealed its hidden value.

**I could:**

- Convert it into a single-family home
- Use it as student housing
- Rent it out room-by-room
- Turn it into an Airbnb
- Develop it into a triplex

With so many options, I negotiated a purchase price of $70,000 *during the pandemic.* I chose the Airbnb route. I invested $15,000 of my own money and financed the rest. Renovations created a 5-bedroom, 2-bath vacation rental that grossed over $70,000 in just 16 months.

That's over 400% ROI in under two years. That's vision.

Five other investors called the realtor *after* I put it under contract. Most of them were from the Daytona Beach area, but they didn't see what I saw – because it was hidden for *me (Thank you, Lord).*

When you start seeing what others cannot see, you will step into blessings others will never walk in.

---

**Poem: Now I Will SEE**

***By Dr. Leon K. McCray – Copyright Protected***

**Immaturity will often look at the imperfection
Immaturity will cause one really to never see past the shell
Immaturity never goes beyond that which is not seen
Immaturity can't go in, it stays locked at the outer court.**

**Oh but look closer, for there's something priceless tucked away inside
No, I can't go in
You see, I've never been inside before
Oh I've peered through at times, as one that looketh through a gate
But I couldn't, I, I wouldn't
You see, I had become comfortable outside.**

**But when God lifts the veil
When he melts away the hurts
And cuts away the past
When immaturity is shaken
Shaken down to its foundational roots
You peek in, come closer.**

**For it's My inner court that you need
My hands have been outstretched
I've beckon you to come in
Come in my child, for in My inner court you will find peace.**

**You've searched for love
You have searched for joy
Yet you've never come in
You stop short at the door.**

**But now you have come, at the lifting of the veil
Glory rise, Glory rise
It's that treasured pearl you see
It's spinning, it's perfect
It's been crafted
Now I will SEE!**

**A Landlord's Superpower: The Ability to See**

**The Litter Box Lesson (A true story)**

I was managing a five-unit building. A potential tenant applied for a 2-bed/1-bath unit. She worked full-time, had a kid, and a friend ready to help with rent. On move-in day, she mentions – for the first time – an "emotional support" dog with a doctor's note. My lease required prior disclosure and written approval for any animal, but the unit was already off the market and she had a kid and boxes. I allowed it.

**Red flag #1:** The last-minute disclosure.
**Red flag #2:** The documentation looked… flimsy. A few weeks later, a plumbing issue gave me reason to visit with my technician. Ten minutes passed before they opened the door.

**Red flag #3:** The place looked fine – except one bedroom stayed "off limits."

**Red flag #4:** Second maintenance visit, same delay at the door. The access panel for the bathroom was in that same bedroom. Inside, I noticed something odd. I lifted the bed skirt – a litter box. My policy: no cats, ever. I took a timestamped photo and said nothing.

On the next visit, I quietly checked again. Same litter box, same spot; second photo.

When I called to asked (gently) about any other animals in the unit, I was told "absolutely not." On court day, the tenant insisted there was no cat, and the dog letter was valid. I presented two photos– bed, box, litter, timestamps. The judge ruled for lease violation. Eviction granted.

In the moment, it felt like a horror story. Looking back, it became training. Seeing what others can't see isn't about suspicion; it's about patterns, documentation, and stewardship (protect your investment).

---

**What This Teaches (Fast Takeaways)**

- Trust… and verify. Compassion first; documentation always.
- Patterns speak. Repeated delays, closed rooms, last-minute "ESA" notes– those add up.
- Your best leverage is process. Clear lease language + consistent screenings + inspections.
- Protect the asset, not your ego. Stay calm, be fair, keep records, and let the paper do the talking.

**Seeing what others can't see is really about positioning:** position your eyes, your process, and your paperwork.

**Let this be your invitation:**
Look again.
Listen again.
Ask God to open your eyes again.

---

Now that your vision is activated, you're ready for the next level – to see how it connects to what's happening in the world around you. Because if you think AI, real estate trends, and economic shifts are random – think again.

They're not just news.

They're **notifications from heaven** that it's time to **pivot, position, and prosper**. See why in the details of **Chapter 7 AI, Real Estate & the Rise of the Renter Nation**

# Chapter 7 AI, Real Estate & the Rise of the Renter Nation

*Seeing What Others Can't See*

---

**Welcome to the New Era**

Imagine waking up and learning your job has been replaced by an algorithm.
The email? Already written.
The design? Already generated.
The Zoom call? Scheduled, completed, and followed up – by AI.

**Welcome to the age of artificial intelligence.**

This isn't the future. This is **now**.
And while some people panic, Kingdom-minded people **prepare** – because we were **built for this**.

---

**The AI Tsunami**

AI is already disrupting:

- Marketing
- Medicine
- Education
- Transportation
- Law
- Real Estate

Jobs are being eliminated.
Tasks are being automated.
Industries are being recreated.

But you're not called to fear disruption – you're called to **lead in the middle of it**.

God is using AI to shift the marketplace, not to push believers out – but to **pull Kingdom thinkers in**.

---

**Rise of the Renter Nation**

Here's what's happening:

Developers are building entire **build-to-rent** communities
Wall Street and institutional investors are buying up homes – not to sell, but to **control them through rentals**

- Americans are renting longer and buying less
  Homeownership is increasingly out of reach for the average family
- This is not just economics – this is **systemic strategy**.
- The American Dream is being leased.
- And if you don't **see what others can't see**, you'll accept it instead of **arising in authority**.

**Think about this: In (Luke 16)**, Jesus tells a parable of a shrewd manager. Now the man was dishonest, but he was also strategic. **And Jesus shocked His listeners when He said that the children of this world are more shrewd than the children of light**.

That word *shrewd* means wise, savvy, sharp in judgment. In Hebrew it means sensible, prudent. In Greek, the word is *phronimos* – wise. **Here's the revelation:** Jesus is not praising dishonesty; **He is praising foresight**. He is telling us that **Kingdom people should never be out-thought, out-planned, or out-positioned by the world**.

When Wall Street is buying up neighborhoods, when corporations are turning homes into rentals, when AI is reshaping industries – the world is moving with strategy. But too often the church is sitting still. The lesson is clear: if we want to win in this season, we need to see what others cannot see. We need to be shrewd, not shady. Wise, not passive. Strategic, not stuck.

The world might be setting up systems to profit, but we as Kingdom people set up systems to prosper and advance the Kingdom.

**This isn't just about survival. This is about stewardship. It's about multiplying what's in our hand, leveraging opportunities, and creating generational wealth with Kingdom purpose. The children of light must rise up wiser than the world – and when we do, we won't just own property, we'll own vision, influence, and legacy.**

---

**What Believers Must Do:** The Kingdom Pivot Plan

- This isn't the time to shrink.
  This is the time to **shine**.
- You were made for this moment.
- You were created to create, assigned to build, and chosen to multiply.
- **Jesus is still King. God is still on the throne. The Spirit is still guiding.**

**Here's how to move now:**

---

**1. Think Like a Producer – Not Just a Consumer**

You weren't designed to just "get by."
You were designed to **dominate**.

You're a **Kingdom producer** – with divine wisdom, spiritual discernment, and marketplace authority.

*"But thou shalt remember the Lord thy God: for it is he that giveth thee power to get wealth…" – (Deuteronomy 8:18)*

That power is still active.
It's your turn to use it.

**2. Use AI as a Kingdom Tool**

AI isn't evil – it's neutral.
It depends on whose hands it's in.

In YOUR hands, it becomes:

- A business builder
- A business partner
- A time saver
- A real estate analyzer
- A marketing assistant
- A prophetic productivity tool

Let the world catch up – you stay ahead.

---

**3. Buy, Build, or Partner – Don't Sit Idle**

Ownership may look different in this season. That's okay.
Start with a single-family home, duplex, a subject-to, a house-hack, building lot or a partnership. **Buy Assets, Buy Assets, Buy Assets.**

You don't have to own everything – but you must **own something**.

Even one property gives you:

- Leverage
- Cash flow
- Tax benefits
- Generational impact

The system may want you to rent forever.
But God called you to **steward land**. **Buy Assets, Buy Assets, Buy Assets.**

### 4. Learn the New Rules – and Master Them

AI, crypto, interest rates, zoning laws, inflation –
It's your job to **learn**, **adjust**, and **move**.

The Kingdom doesn't wait for the world to teach us.
We move by revelation **and** information.

---

### 5. Own Something – No Matter What

You may rent your apartment…
But you should never rent:

- Your identity
- Your purpose
- Your mission
- Your mindset

**Own your brand.**
**Own your vision.**
**Own your part in God's unfolding plan.**

*"The earth is the Lord's… and He gave it to the children of men." – (Psalm 115:16)*

**Buy Assets, Buy Assets, Buy Assets**

---

### 6. Don't Just Dream – BUILD

This isn't the time to wait and wonder.

It's the time to:

- Move in faith
- Partner with wisdom

- Use the tools
- Hear from God
- Build your ark before the rain

You are a Kingdom innovator.
A solution-bringer.
A visionary with divine instructions.

---

**The AI x Real Estate Equation**

| **Area** | **Pre-AI Era** | **AI-Driven World** |
|---|---|---|
| Work | Labor + Time | Value + Insight |
| Real Estate | Buy and Hold / Flip | Rent-to-Own, Short-Term Rentals, BTR |
| Learning | Traditional School | Self-Education + AI-Powered Tools |
| Marketing | Flyers and Manual Ads | AI-Funnels + Automation |
| Wealth Building | Slow and Safe | Supercharged w/ Kingdom + Tech |
| Faith Integration | Sunday-Only Faith | Everyday Application |

---

**Final Word: Vision + Action = Victory**

You've now seen what others overlook:

- The power of vision and insight
- The shift in the economy

- The rise of renter culture
- And the door opening for Kingdom entrepreneurs

**This is your time.**
Not to escape… but to **engage**.
Not to worry… but to **worship while you work**.

God is still speaking.
Jesus is still saving.
And you are still being sent.

It's time to **see what others cannot see** –
… and **build what others cannot build**.

Don't back up, don't back down, **buy Assets, and advance the kingdom.**

---

**The Future Outlook**

"If you think the pace of change is fast now, hold on. The next 10 years will make the last 10 look like a warm-up lap."

- Technology is advancing at an exponential rate, transforming industries faster than regulations or traditions can keep up.
- **The balance of wealth is shifting** – away from labor and toward those who own and control **income-producing assets**.
- **Artificial Intelligence is not coming… it's already here**, and it will impact how we work, live, and compete in the marketplace.
- Globalization means your competitor or collaborator could be halfway across the world – and still be part of your market.
- **The real winners will be those who see these shifts early and adapt rather than resist**.

---

**AI: The Game Changer**

"AI is not just another technological upgrade – **it's the next industrial revolution**."

- Companies are using AI to automate processes, increase efficiency, and cut costs dramatically.
- Decision-making is becoming more data-driven and less gut-driven – meaning **the edge will belong to those who can harness AI tools effectively**.
- The best part? **AI levels the playing field – a small business owner with AI can compete with a company 10 times their size**.
- But here's the warning: Those who ignore AI risk becoming irrelevant in their industry.

---

**The AI Job Impact**

"Let's be real – AI will disrupt jobs, but it will also create massive opportunity."

- Studies suggest that **up to 50% of jobs** could be automated in some form within a decade.
- High-value positions in management, legal, design, and media will be reshaped – not just entry-level roles.
- The **key to surviving** this shift is **reskilling** – learning **how to work alongside AI** rather than be replaced by it.
- **Entrepreneurs and investors who understand AI will be able to scale faster, serve more customers, and dominate new markets**.

---

**Opportunities Others Miss**

"While most people are panicking about change, **visionaries are preparing to profit from it**."

- Invest in AI-related businesses and infrastructure before they hit mass adoption.
- **Acquire** both **digital assets** (like intellectual property, AI tools, online platforms) and **hard assets** (like real estate) before demand spikes.
- Use AI to automate marketing, streamline operations, and personalize customer experiences.
- **Look for industries on the verge of exponential growth** – these are often where the greatest wealth transfers happen.

---

**The "Wealth Code" Unlocked in the AI Era**

"This is where faith meets foresight."

- Faith allows you to move boldly into new territory without fear.
- **Vision allows you to anticipate shifts in the market before they become mainstream**.
- Stewardship ensures that when increase comes, you manage and multiply it for long-term impact.
- The goal isn't just personal wealth – it's Kingdom advancement. We're here to build influence, create opportunities, and fund the future.

---

**AI as the New Real Estate**

- In real estate, the wealth is not just in owning the land but in how you **develop, manage, and leverage it.**

- AI is no different. Right now, it's wide-open land - some is raw dirt, some is fertile soil, and some already has "skyscrapers" going up (think Google, Microsoft, OpenAI).
- **Just like a smart investor, Kingdom Believers must discern:** ***Where do I buy in? Where do I build? Where do I hold?***

---

**How Kingdom Believers Position Themselves**

**1. Own the Mindset Before You Own the Tools**

- (Proverbs 4:7): *"Wisdom is the principal thing; therefore get wisdom."*
- Before jumping into AI out of hype, develop the mindset that AI is a **tool of stewardship, multiplication, and dominion** – not a gimmick, not a threat.
- The early adopters will be the ones who shape culture with it.

---

**2. Claim Territory Through Creation, Not Just Consumption**

- In real estate, renters consume space; owners create space.
- Many will "rent AI" by just using apps others build. Kingdom Believers must **own AI spaces** – by building applications, writing books, teaching courses, automating businesses, and setting up systems that multiply.
- Ask: *Am I renting the technology, or am I creating with it?*

---

**3. Leverage AI to Multiply Kingdom Assignments**

- AI can draft contracts, analyze deals, generate marketing, and even simulate market scenarios.
- That means one Kingdom entrepreneur with vision can now do the work of ten people.

- The wealth shift will go to those who know how to **multiply output without multiplying overhead.**

---

### 4. Partner With AI Like You Partner With Real Estate

- Real estate has tenants, managers, and contractors. You don't do everything yourself.
- Treat AI the same way – it's your new "assistant," "analyst," "writer," and "researcher."
- Don't fear it – employ **it. Make it work for you**.

---

### 5. Build Systems That Outlive You

- Just as real estate produces **cash flow and legacy**, AI systems can produce **information flow and influence** long after you're gone.
- Imagine an AI-powered training system that teaches your principles to future generations, or an AI model trained on Kingdom stewardship. That's legacy thinking.

---

### The Kingdom Advantage

The world is already staking claim on AI like land developers. But here's the difference:

- They build for profit.
- We build for **purpose.**
- They use it to control markets.
- We use it to **advance the Kingdom.**

AI is the "new real estate," and the Kingdom play is to see it, seize it, and steward it before the world monopolizes it.

---

In short: **Kingdom Believers must stop renting!**

### Action Steps for the Next Decade

"The next decade is going to be a defining moment – for nations, for businesses, and for individuals. **Here's how you prepare**."

1. **Develop AI literacy now** – even a **basic understanding puts you ahead of 90% of people**.
2. **Identify industries with high growth potential** – especially those that can't be easily automated.
3. **Invest in scalable, tech-enabled assets** – businesses, platforms, and properties that can grow without more hours from you.
4. **Build multiple streams of income** – rely on more than one source so you're never at the mercy of a single employer or market shift.
5. **Stay flexible and teachable** – the ability to pivot quickly will be more valuable than a decade of experience in a fading industry.

Throughout this book, we've unlocked the truth that wealth is not just a number in a bank account – it's a mindset, a strategy, and a stewardship mandate. We've seen that the real **"Wealth Code" Unlocked** is built on three pillars:

1. **Faith** – Believing that you were created for dominion, provision, and impact.
2. **Vision** – Seeing opportunities others miss and positioning yourself ahead of the curve.
3. **Action** – Building, acquiring, and multiplying assets that produce freedom and legacy.

We've explored how to navigate a shifting economy, why *assets* are the key to financial increase, and how AI and technological change are rewriting the rules of wealth creation. While the world is bracing for disruption, those who can see what others cannot, will thrive – not just survive.

But here's the truth:
**The code is only unlocked** when you **apply** it. Knowledge without action is just potential. Your financial future will not change because you read this book – it will change because you decided to move, to invest, to steward, and to multiply.

---

The conclusion is your invitation to step fully into this new reality – to live as one who has unlocked the code and refuses to settle for average. The next move is yours, and the moment is now.

Let's talk about how you can take everything you've learned and **activate your "Wealth Code" Unlocked** starting today.

---

# CONCLUSION

## *"The Wealth Code" Unlocked*

## Your New Chapter Begins

---

**You've reached the end of these pages**, but you're standing at the threshold of a brand-new chapter. **This isn't an ending – it's a beginning.** What you've received is more than strategies and market insights. **You've been entrusted with a revelation - truths that were never meant to be locked away, but placed in the hands of those ready to steward them well.** You've been given a key that unlocks more than money.

**The "Wealth Code" Unlocked** has never been just about money. **It's about identity, legacy, and purpose - knowing who you are in God, why you're here, and what you're called to build and leave behind.**

### The Code Is in Your Hands

You now carry the double key: the ability to unlock financial opportunity and the deeper spiritual identity that governs how you handle it. **You've learned the principles the world's wealthiest quietly live by – build, multiply, protect – and advance something greater than yourself.** Now those same keys are in your hand.

**We're living in an opportunity-rich, disruptive moment.** AI is reshaping industries. Wall Street is redrawing real estate. **Wealth is shifting hands. People with vision, courage, and Kingdom stewardship won't just survive this moment – they'll define it.**

### Your "Wealth Code" Unlocked Mindset

- Faith is your ceiling. Believe small, live small. **Believe big, live big**.
- Vision is your compass. **What you see determines where you arrive.**
- **Action is your key**. Revelation unused becomes regret.

**Tithing opens the windows of heaven** (Malachi 3:10), **but stewardship of the 90% decides what flows through them.** The wealthy don't wait for permission– they prepare. **While others see crisis, they see opportunity**. While others freeze, they move**. While others spend, they acquire.**

---

**From My Story to Yours**

**As I shared in the introduction**, I never met my biological father. That's a reality I've made peace with – yet **in God's divine plan, He allowed me to meet Airman Parker, a man who became the bridge to the most life-changing meeting of my life: my introduction to my ****real Father*** – **my Heavenly Father** – and His Son, **Jesus Christ**.

That encounter unlocked something in me that no business deal, investment, or achievement could ever touch. **It answered questions I'd carried for decades and released a deeper understanding of who I am, whose I am, and what I was born to build.**

I realized the true **"Wealth Code" Unlocked** was never just about assets – **it was about being a son of the King, operating in Kingdom authority, and leaving a legacy that outlives me**.

And now, **you stand where I once stood** – key **in hand**, ready to unlock what God has placed in you.

**Seven Bold Moves to Activate the Code**

1. **Write the Vision (Habakkuk 2:2).** Define life, legacy, industry impact, and Kingdom assignment.

2. **Move This Week.** Call the lender, register the LLC, buy the asset, meet the mentor/coach. **Movement births momentum.**
3. **Steward What's in Your Hand (Luke 16:10).** Faithfulness attracts increase.
4. **Embrace AI & Tools.** Multiply impact; don't fear the moment – lead it.
5. **Build Your Power Team.** People who amplify your vision and sharpen your execution.
6. **Multiply What Works – Release** What Doesn't. Focus on proven returns; cut the drains.
7. **Keep the Kingdom First (Matthew 6:33).** Let mission govern money, not the other way around.

**Your Declaration**

**From this day forward:**
I will see what others cannot see.
I will build what others fear to build.
I will steward faithfully what God places in my hands.
I will leave a legacy of faith, impact, and abundance.
I will walk daily in wisdom, wealth, and Kingdom authority.

**Final Charge**

The keys are in your hand. Go. Build. Multiply. Advance the Kingdom. Live boldly.

***"Beloved, I wish above all things that thou mayest prosper and be in health, even as thy soul prospereth." – (3 John 2)***

May wisdom guide your decisions, favor open the right doors, diligence keep you steady, and generosity keep your heart free. Your life, your legacy, and your lineage are waiting on the other side of your obedience.

Thank you for walking with me this far. It has been - my great honor to serve you, my friend. I'm humbled – and deeply grateful that you chose to lean in, reflect, and do the hard inner work. Align your heart, your habits, and your hustle with God's purpose for your life. **The "Wealth Code" is UNLOCKED to YOU. BLESSINGS**

## My Prayer to Release You into Your Destiny

Father, in the mighty name of Jesus, I lift up every reader who has journeyed through these pages. Lord, they have received not just information, but revelation. They now carry the keys of wisdom, identity, and authority that unlock wealth, purpose, and legacy. I declare that these keys will not remain idle in their hands, but will activate movements, multiply opportunities, and open doors no man can shut.

Lord, I pray that faith rises in them like never before – bold faith that dreams beyond limitations, believes beyond fear, and acts with Heaven's confidence. Let vision ignite like fire in their hearts, illuminating paths where others see only obstacles. And let courage propel them into new territory, unafraid to build, unafraid to lead, unafraid to steward the inheritance You have placed within them.

Father, as they step forward, let the "Wealth Code" within them come alive. Cause their hands to prosper, their minds to sharpen, and their spirits to discern what others cannot see. May they steward resources with honor, multiply what works, and release what hinders. May they build teams, strategies, and systems that advance not just their dreams, but Your Kingdom.

Lord, release divine favor over their lives. Let contracts, connections, and opportunities align by Your hand. Let wisdom be their guide, diligence be their strength, generosity be their shield, and integrity be their foundation.

I declare over them: they will not be bound by scarcity, fear, or the lies of the enemy. They will move with divine acceleration. They will write the vision, run with it, and finish well. They will leave a legacy of faith, wealth, and impact that echoes for generations to come.

Now, Lord, send them out. Energized. Equipped. Empowered. Ready to build boldly, multiply faithfully, and advance the Kingdom with unstoppable force. May their lives be living testimonies of (3 John 2): *"Beloved, I wish above all things that thou mayest prosper and be in health, even as thy soul prospereth."*

Father, I thank You for the honor of pouring into them. Now I release them into the destiny for which they were created. The "Wealth Code" is unlocked. The time is now. The Kingdom is advancing. And these, Your sons and daughters, will run with fire.

**In *Jesus'* mighty name, Amen.**

# Acknowledgements

# Acknowledgements

**When I think about my wife, my *Queen, Dr. Valerie Anne McCray***, my heart overflows with gratitude. I am in awe of how the Lord has favored me – that He would place you in my life as a living testimony of His supernatural goodness. Truly, only God could give such a gift. Valerie, you are incredibly beautiful, full of grace, and steadfast in your call to serve the men and women of God. You not only chose to walk with me, but you saw in me what others could not see. To become my wife - and the devoted mother of our two young sons - required courage, faith, and vision. You embody all three in abundance. Though this is written as an acknowledgment, it is truly also **a dedication**. Because without you, babe, I would not be at this juncture in life. Your powerful prayers, your **prophetic mantle**, your intercession - they have been a guiding light, a covering that has carried me through. From those prayers was birthed what is now called **The Lighthouse** - the merging of my vision and your vision, united as one by the Mighty Hand of God.

I am honored to serve with you in ministry, to walk beside you as we travel the world, and to present you as my Pearl to the Nations. Together, we are called to build and advance the Kingdom of God, to bring heaven to earth, and to fulfill our divine destiny and calling. Only the "Resurrected King of Glory" could have written such a story for us - and I am forever grateful to live it with you.

---

***To my daughters, Celena and Shauntae:*** You are my jewels – precious, radiant, and entrusted with a beauty and strength that comes from God. Every gift He has placed in you will flourish in due season – to fulfil your purpose and to leave a legacy for your family. Continue to walk in wisdom, grace, and courage as the Kingdom Daughters, He has called you to be. Your love and faithful support mean more than words can express. I LOVE YOU BOTH SO VERY MUCH.

***To my sons, Leon (LJ) and Uriah:*** You are pillars – strong, steady, and called to be builders in the Kingdom of God. Every word spoken over your lives will come to pass in God's perfect timing. Keep pressing forward, walking in wisdom, and growing into the men and fathers He has called you to be. You carry a light that will shine brightly as you fulfill your purpose. MY LOVE FOR YOU IS VERY DEEPLY ROOTED.

---

***To my Fourteen Grandchildren:*** Corey, Alexus, Marquet, Destiny, Noah, Aamori, Isaiah, Royal, Kamaiah (Leona), Willow, and Jayleigh - and my three great-granddaughters, Kennedy, Gianna (LeGianna), and Sunflower: Each of you inspire me daily to be the best Pop-Pop I can be. My constant prayer is that I reflect and reveal Christ, the Resurrected King of Glory, in a way that leaves you a legacy of faith, love, and strength - one that propels you toward fulfilling your Kingdom purpose. I LOVE YOU'LL SO MUCH.

---

***To my siblings, Glenn and Frances (Nae Nae), and my other brother Tony:*** Thank you for being my support system, lifting my spirit, and encouraging me always. Family is everything. Your prayers, love, and countless conversations have been a source of joy and strength. I LOVE YOU'LL MORE THAN WORDS CAN SAY.

---

***To Prophet Dr. Tony Robertson:*** Your encouragement, prayers, and unwavering friendship have meant more to me than words can capture. For over two decades, you have walked with me, witnessed my journey, and seen the hand of God unfold in my life and ministry. You know my character, my calling, and the pivotal moments that shaped the very heart of this book. Your willingness to write the Foreword is more than an honor - it is a reflection of the steadfast support and covering you have always given. Thank you for your love, standing with me, believing in me, and affirming the work God has called me to do. I am deeply grateful and love you so very much.

---

***Apostle Desiree Fox***, our Regional Director and Overseer of Lighthouse Marketplace Ministries: you are our Momma Eagle, nurturing yet fierce, always just a call or visit away. Your keen prophetic insight, wisdom, and guidance have kept us aligned with God's will. Your encouragement and love have been invaluable, and we deeply love and honor you. We also honor the memory and legacy of your late husband, **Apostle Guy Fox**, whose faith, strength, and devotion to the Kingdom continue to inspire us all. Together, your lives and ministries have left an indelible mark for the glory of God.

---

***Apostle Dr. Tony and Dr. Sharlene Barhoo***, my amazing pastors**:** Thank you for receiving my wife and me into the Living Faith World Ministries Family with such love and honor. We know God divinely planted us under your covering, and we are grateful for your leadership, wisdom, and vision that continually elevate and equip us for greater service in His Kingdom. Your powerful teachings stir our spirits, deepen our faith, and challenge us to grow in maturity and excellence. Thank you for your love, trust, and inspiration, and for guiding us to walk faithfully. We love and honor you both, giving all glory to God for this journey we share together.

---

## Tribute to the Lighthouse

**Father,** thank You for trusting us with the **Lighthouse**.

Before there was a blueprint or a budget, You lit a flame in my spirit. Twenty-five years ago, when **"Marketplace Ministry"** was hardly spoken of, You showed my wife and me a house of light– rooms for training and counseling, places to eat and gather, boutiques and businesses that serve with integrity, a living center where ministry and enterprise stand side by side under the lordship of Jesus. We had no roadmap and no mentor, only Your voice and the nudge of the Holy Spirit. Yet that was enough. Your light went before us.

You made the **Lighthouse** an incubator - first for us, then for the work. In hidden seasons You formed our character, enlarged our compassion, and taught us to shepherd people and steward resources. Like the seed in (Mark 4), the Kingdom grew "all by itself"- first the blade, then the head, then the full grain (Mark 4:26–29). You planted prosperity and purpose in my inner man; You asked me to water what You planted with obedience and diligence, and then You brought the increase.

I remember the word You spoke over me more than two decades ago. I honored it then; I've revisited it often. But lately, as I write, it feels like the page reads me - the lines leaping up with fresh breath. It was never merely a prediction; it has become our lived testimony. You said You would breathe on my mind and give me images, ideas, and understanding in hours I knew not of. You whispered that imagination, baptized by Your Spirit, can carry blueprints that knowledge alone cannot hold. You promised wisdom and the wind of Your Spirit on the work of my hands. Truly, it is You who gives me the power to get wealth, to establish Your covenant (Deuteronomy 8:18).

You set us in the marketplace on purpose, to stand among leaders and wealth-holders and call them to build the Kingdom again. You gave discernment to know light from darkness (Malachi 3:16–18) and courage to say, "Come, let us rise and build." You spoke of blessings, long dormant ruins to be raised, ancient wells to be reopened, and You have been faithful to resurrect what seemed lost and to root it in righteousness (Isaiah 61:4).

And so, this **Lighthouse** is more than a building; it is a people and a posture. It is a promise that in storms we will keep the lens clean and the flame bright. It is a vow to serve the searching, to counsel the weary, to train and employ, to preach good news without apology, to transact with integrity, and to turn profit into purpose. It is our yes to being a city on a hill, seen not for our glory, but for Yours (Matthew 5:14–16).

Thank You for every night You taught my heart while I slept, for every open door and every closed one, for correction that guarded us and favor that carried us. Thank You for Valerie, my covenant partner in this assignment, whose prayers, strength, and prophetic insight have steadied my hands on the lantern. Thank You for every person You've sent to build, to give, to learn, to heal, to be healed. Every testimony is a beam in this tower.

**Now, Father, do again what only You can do:**

- Let Your light reach farther than our plans.
- Let nations and neighborhoods walk toward the glow (Isaiah 60:1–3).
- Let Your wind drive the beam through fog and fear.
- Let wisdom, creativity, and holy imagination keep expanding the work.

- Let wealth be a servant of Your will and a witness to Your goodness.

I consecrate the **Lighthouse** afresh to You. Make it a safe harbor and a bold signal, an engine for equipping and a home for healing. Keep us small in our own eyes and large in our obedience. May every room hum with Your presence, and every ledger line testify that Jesus is Lord.

All the honor belongs to You, Father.
All the light is Yours.
All the increase is Yours.

Soli Deo Gloria.

*Apostle, Dr. Leon K. McCray*
*Founder, Lighthouse Marketplace Ministries*

**"Wealth Code" Unlocked**

Thank you for investing the time to read *"Wealth Code" Unlocked.* It is my sincere prayer that the principles, insights, and strategies shared in this book have strengthened your financial literacy, expanded your vision for wealth, and encouraged purposeful stewardship for generations to come.

**Connect with the Author**

If you would like to share your comments, reflections, or how this book has impacted your wealth-building journey, please feel free to reach out:

**Email:**
leonkmccray@gmail.com

**Continue the Journey**

To purchase additional copies, explore related resources, or share this message with a friend, please visit:

www.Amazon.com

www.wealthcodeinstitute.com

You may also scan the QR code below for direct access to the website.

www.ingramcontent.com/pod-product-compliance
Lightning Source LLC
LaVergne TN
LVHW020716110826
845149LV00012B/2286

*9798994483206*